Agatha Christie

They Do It With Mirrors

Collins

Collins

HarperCollins Publishers
77-85 Fulham Palace Road
Hammersmith, London W6 8JB
www.collinselt.com

This *Collins English Readers Edition* published 2012

Reprint 10 9 8 7 6 5 4 3 2 1 0

First published in Great Britain by Collins 1952

ISBN: 978-85-7827-530-3

A catalogue record for this book is available from the British Library.

Cover by crushed.co.uk © HarperCollins/Agatha Christie Ltd 2008

Typeset by Aptara in India

Printed and bound in Great Britain by Clays Ltd, St Ives plc

Contents

Story	1
Character list	102
Cultural notes	104
Glossary	107

Chapter 1

Ruth Van Rydock was beautifully dressed. Her face, with its expensive make-up, appeared almost girlish at a distance. Her hair was more blue than grey and perfectly styled. Everything that money could do for Mrs Van Rydock had been done.

Ruth Van Rydock smiled at her friend. 'Do you think most people would guess, Jane, that you and I are the same age?'

Miss Marple answered loyally. 'Not for a moment, I'm sure. I'm afraid, you know, that I look every day of my age!'

Miss Marple was white-haired, with a soft, pink and white wrinkled face and innocent blue eyes. She looked a very sweet old lady. Nobody would have called Mrs Van Rydock a sweet old lady.

'I guess you do, Jane,' said Mrs Van Rydock. She grinned suddenly, 'And so do I. Only not in the same way.' She sat on a silk-covered chair. 'Jane, I want to talk to you.'

Miss Marple leant forward to listen carefully. She looked out of place in this grand bedroom of an expensive hotel, dressed as she was in old-fashioned black and carrying a large shopping bag.

'I'm worried, Jane. About Carrie Louise.'

'Carrie Louise?' Miss Marple repeated. Oh, the name took her a long way back, to the exciting days before the First World War when she was a student in Florence, sharing an apartment with two American sisters. They had been very different to young Jane Marple, quietly brought up in a gentle English cathedral town. Ruth was tall and full of energy while Carrie Louise was small, delicate and dreamy, but both had that direct American way of talking and she had liked them at once.

'When did you last see Carrie Louise, Jane?'

'Oh! Not for many years. Of course we still send cards at Christmas.'

Such a strange thing, friendship! She, young Jane Marple, and the two Americans, had separated after school, and yet the old affection was still there. And it was strange that Ruth, whose home – or rather homes – had been in America, was the sister Jane had seen more often. No, perhaps not strange. Every year or two Ruth had come over to Europe, rushing from London to Paris, on to the Riviera, and back again, but she always saw her old friends. There had been many affectionate meetings like this one.

However, Jane had not seen Carrie Louise for twenty years, although Carrie Louise lived in England. But this was natural, because when you live in the same country as an old friend, but have very different lives, you do not meet. The paths of Jane Marple and Carrie Louise did not cross. It was as simple as that.

'Why are you worried about Carrie Louise, Ruth?' asked Miss Marple.

'In a way, that's what worries me most! I don't know.'

'She's not ill?'

'She's very delicate – always has been. But no worse than usual.'

'Unhappy?'

'Oh no.'

No, it wouldn't be that, thought Miss Marple. It was difficult to imagine Carrie Louise being unhappy.

'Carrie Louise,' said Ruth Van Rydock, 'has always believed that everyone is like her: good-natured and with a kind heart. She was always the one of us who had ideals. Of course it was the fashion when we were young to have ideals – we all had them; it was the proper thing for young girls. You were going to nurse lepers, Jane, and I was going to be a nun. But we got over all that nonsense. Marriage certainly makes you face the real world. Still, marriage has worked well for me.'

That was true, thought Miss Marple. Ruth had been married three times, each time to a wealthy man, and each divorce had increased her bank balance without making her in the least bitter.

'Of course,' said Mrs Van Rydock, 'I've always been tough. I've not expected too much of men – and had no regrets. Tommy and I are still excellent friends, and Julius often asks me my opinion about business.' She frowned. 'I believe that's what worries me about Carrie Louise – she's always had a tendency, you know, to marry cranks.'

'Cranks?'

'Adults with ideals. Carrie Louise was always impressed by ideals. There she was, as pretty as can be, just seventeen and listening with her eyes wide to old Gulbrandsen, talking about his plans for the human race. He was over fifty, and she married him, a widower with a family of grown-up children – all because of his philanthropic ideas.

Miss Marple nodded thoughtfully. The name of Gulbrandsen was known internationally; a man who had earned a huge fortune and then used it to create many great charitable organizations.

'She didn't marry him for his money, you know,' said Ruth, 'I would have. But not Carrie Louise. And then he died when she was thirty-two. But then I really was happiest about Carrie Louise when she was married to Johnnie Restarick. Of course he *did* marry her for her money. Johnnie was lazy, and pleasure-loving, but that's so much safer than being a crank. All Johnnie wanted was to live well and for Carrie Louise to enjoy herself. That kind of man is so very safe. Give him comfort and luxury and he'll purr like a cat. I never took that theatrical designing of his very seriously. But Carrie Louise loved it – she thought it was very artistic work and wanted him to go back into the theatre, and then that terrible Yugoslavian woman got hold of him and took him away.'

'Was Carrie Louise very upset?' asked Miss Marple.

'I don't believe she was. She was absolutely sweet about it – but then she *is* sweet. She gave Alex and Stephen, Johnnie's sons by his first marriage, a home with her. And that Yugoslavian woman gave Johnnie a terrible six months and then, in a temper, drove him over a cliff in a car!'

Mrs Van Rydock paused. 'And what does Carrie Louise do next, but marry this man Lewis Serrocold. Another crank! Another man with ideals! Oh, he certainly loves her – but he also wants to improve everybody's lives for them. And really, you know, nobody can do that for you – you have to do it yourself.'

'I wonder,' said Miss Marple.

'Only, of course, there's a fashion in philanthropy, just like there is in clothes. It used to be "education for all" in Gulbrandsen's time. But that's out of date. The government does that now. Everyone expects education as a right – and doesn't think much of it when they get it! Juvenile delinquency is the top fashion nowadays. All these young criminals – everyone's mad about them. You should see Lewis Serrocold's eyes shine behind those thick glasses of his. Mad with enthusiasm! He is one of those men with huge willpower who likes living on a banana and a piece of toast and puts all their energies into a cause. And Carrie Louise loves it – just as she always did. But I don't like it, Jane. They've had meetings of the trustees and Stonygates is now a training establishment for juvenile criminals, full of boys who aren't normal, with psychiatrists and psychologists and occupational therapists and teachers, half of them quite mad. Cranks, the lot of them, and my little Carrie Louise is in the middle of it all!' She paused – and stared helplessly at Miss Marple.

Miss Marple said, 'But you haven't told me yet, Ruth, what you are really afraid of.'

'I tell you, I don't know! And that's what worries me. I've just been down to Stonygates and I felt there was something wrong. But I don't know if it's these young criminals, or if it's something more personal. I can't say what it is. And I want you, Jane, to go down there right away and find out exactly what is wrong.'

'Me?' exclaimed Miss Marple. 'Why me?'

'Because you know about these things, Jane. Nothing has ever surprised you, you always believe the worst.'

'The worst is so often true,' said Miss Marple.

'I can't think why you have such a poor opinion of human nature, living in that peaceful village of St Mary Mead.'

'Human nature, dear, is very much the same everywhere. The things that happen in a peaceful village would probably surprise you. It is more difficult to notice them in a city, that is all.'

'My point is that they don't surprise you. So you will go down to Stonygates and find out what's wrong, won't you?'

'But, Ruth dear, that would be most difficult.'

'No, it wouldn't. I've thought it all out. Please don't be angry with me.'

Mrs Van Rydock began a nervous explanation. 'You'll admit, I'm sure, that things have been difficult since the war, for people with small, fixed incomes – for people like you, Jane.'

'Oh yes, indeed. If it wasn't for the great generosity of my nephew Raymond, I really don't know how I would manage with money.'

'Carrie Louise knows nothing about your nephew,' said Mrs Van Rydock. 'The point, as I put it to Carrie Louise, is that it's just too bad about dear Jane. Sometimes she doesn't have enough to eat and she's much too proud to ask old friends for anything. You couldn't offer her money – but a nice long rest in lovely surroundings, with an old friend and with plenty of good food,' Ruth Van Rydock paused and then added, 'Now go on – be angry if you want.'

Miss Marple opened her blue eyes in gentle surprise. 'But why should I be angry at you, Ruth? It was a very good approach. I'm sure Carrie Louise responded.'

'She's writing to you. Honestly, Jane, you don't mind . . . ?'

She hesitated and Miss Marple put her thoughts neatly into words. 'Going to Stonygates and pretending to be in need of charity? Not in the least. You think it is necessary – and I agree with you.'

Mrs Van Rydock stared at her. 'But why? What have you heard?'

'I haven't heard anything. It's you that I trust, Ruth.'

Chapter 2

Before she caught her train back to St Mary Mead, Miss Marple, in a business-like way, asked for details.

'It's just the facts I need, Ruth dear – and some idea of who I will meet at Stonygates.'

'Well, you know about Carrie Louise's marriage to Gulbrandsen. There were no children and Carrie Louise was very upset by that. Gulbrandsen was a widower, and had three grown-up sons. Eventually he and Carrie Louise adopted a child. Pippa, they called her – a lovely little girl just two years old. And the next thing that happened was that Carrie Louise had a baby after all. I understand from doctors that that quite often happens.'

Miss Marple nodded. 'I believe so.'

'Anyway, it did happen, but then their daughter Mildred, when she arrived, was a very unattractive child. She looked like the Gulbrandsens, who are good people but very plain. Carrie Louise was so anxious to make no difference between the adopted child and her own that I think she gave even more attention to Pippa – which made Mildred unhappy. Pippa grew up a very beautiful girl and Mildred grew up a plain one. Gulbrandsen left an equal amount of money to both daughters – and at twenty Pippa married an Italian aristocrat. Mildred married Canon Strete – a nice man, but he often had colds in the head. He was about fifteen years older than she was. It was quite a happy marriage, I believe.

'He died a year ago and Mildred has come back to Stonygates to live with her mother. But I've missed a marriage or two. I'll go back to them. Pippa married her Italian, Guido. A year later

Pippa had a daughter called Gina and died in childbirth. It was a terrible tragedy and Guido was in a very bad way. Carrie Louise went to Italy so very often, to see him and his daughter – and it was in Rome that she met Johnnie Restarick and married him. Guido married again and he was happy for his daughter to be brought up in England by her very wealthy grandmother. So they all lived at Stonygates, Johnnie Restarick and Carrie Louise, and Johnnie's two boys, Alex and Stephen, and the baby Gina. Then came this business with the Yugoslavian woman. But the boys are devoted to Carrie Louise – and then in 1938, Carrie Louise married Lewis Serrocold.' Mrs Van Rydock paused for breath. 'You've not met Lewis?'

Miss Marple shook her head. 'No, I think I last saw Carrie Louise in 1928. She very kindly took me to the opera.'

'Well, Lewis was a very appropriate person. He was the head of a very respectable company of accountants. I think he met her first concerning some questions about the finances of the Gulbrandsen charitable organizations. He was wealthy enough, her own age, and very respectable. But he was a crank. He was absolutely determined to save young criminals.'

Ruth Van Rydock sighed.

'As I said just now, Jane, there are fashions in philanthropy. And the Gulbrandsen Trust and Education Fund was in some difficulties because the government was taking over its functions. Then Lewis came along with his passionate enthusiasm about training for juvenile delinquents. It all began with his work, examining accounts where clever young men had committed frauds. He was sure that juvenile delinquents had good brains and abilities and only needed to be shown the right direction.'

'That is a good idea,' said Miss Marple. 'But it is not entirely true. I remember . . .' She broke off and looked at her watch. 'Oh dear – I mustn't miss the 6.30 train home.'

Ruth Van Rydock said urgently, 'And you will go to Stonygates? Promise, Jane?'

Jane Marple promised.

Chapter 3

Miss Marple got out of the train at Market Kindle station, holding tightly a string bag and an old leather handbag and looking more poorly dressed than usual.

Miss Marple was looking around the windy station – there were no passengers or railway staff anywhere – when a young man came up to her.

'Miss Marple?' His voice had an unexpectedly dramatic quality, as though he was playing a part in a theatre. 'I've come to meet you – from Stonygates.'

The personality of this young man did not match his voice. His loud voice was meant to make him seem important, when in fact he was almost nervous.

'Oh thank you,' said Miss Marple. 'There's just this suitcase.'

The young man raised a hand at a porter who was pushing some large boxes past on a handcart. 'Bring it out, please,' he said, and added importantly, 'for Stonygates.'

'I won't be long,' the porter said cheerfully.

Miss Marple thought that the young man was not too pleased about this delay.

Taking Miss Marple towards the exit, he said, 'I'm Edgar Lawson. Mrs Serrocold asked me to meet you. I help Mr Serrocold in his work.'

He behaved as if he were a busy and important man who had, very charmingly, put important business on one side to be polite to his employer's wife. And again it was not completely successful – it had a theatrical flavour.

Miss Marple began to wonder about Edgar Lawson.

They came out of the station to where a rather old Ford was standing – just then a new two-seater Rolls Bentley came into the station yard and stopped in front of the Ford. A beautiful young woman jumped out. The fact that she wore old trousers and a simple shirt seemed somehow to make it more obvious that she was not only beautiful, but expensive.

'There you are, Edgar. I see you've got Miss Marple. I came to meet her.' She smiled brilliantly at Miss Marple, showing lovely teeth in a sunburnt face. 'I'm Gina,' she said. 'Carrie Louise's granddaughter. What was your journey like? Simply horrible? What a nice string bag. I love string bags. I'll take it and you get in.'

Edgar's face blushed red. He complained. 'Look here, Gina, I came to meet Miss Marple. It was all arranged.'

Again that wide smile. 'Oh I know, Edgar, but I suddenly thought it would be nice if I came. I'll take her with me and you can wait and bring her cases.'

She shut the door on Miss Marple, jumped in the driving seat, and they drove quickly out of the station.

Miss Marple looked back at Edgar Lawson's face. 'I don't think, my dear,' she said, 'that Mr Lawson is very pleased.'

Gina laughed. 'Edgar's such a fool,' she said. 'Always so self-important. He really thinks he is important!'

Miss Marple asked, 'Isn't he important?'

'Edgar?' There was a thoughtless cruelty in Gina's laugh. 'Oh, he's mad anyway.'

'Mad?'

'Oh, you know,' said Gina. 'Crazy. They're all mad at Stonygates. I don't mean Lewis and Grandma and me and the boys – and not Miss Bellever, of course. But the others. Sometimes I feel I'm going a bit mad myself living there.'

Gina gave her a quick sideways look. 'You were at school with Grandma, weren't you?'

'Yes, indeed,' said Miss Marple, thinking of being young and struggling with English literature. 'And it is a long time since I've seen her. I wonder if I'll find her much changed.'

'She walks with a stick because of her arthritis. It's got much worse lately. Have you been to Stonygates before?'

'No.'

'The house is pretty horrible, really,' said Gina cheerfully. 'And everything's very serious, with psychiatrists everywhere. But the young criminals are fun, some of them. One showed me how to open locks with a bit of wire and one child taught me how to knock people out.'

Miss Marple considered this thoughtfully.

'It's the violent ones I like best,' said Gina. 'I don't like the mad ones so much. Of course Lewis and Dr Maverick think they're all mad – I mean they think it's because they've had a bad home life – with mothers who ran away with soldiers and all that. I don't really agree because some people have had terrible home lives and yet have managed to grow up all right.'

'I'm sure it is a difficult problem,' said Miss Marple. 'The young man who met me at the station, is he Mr Serrocold's secretary?'

'Oh Edgar hasn't got enough brains to be a secretary. He's mad, really. He used to stay at hotels and pretend he was an Air Force pilot with medals. He used to borrow money and then run off. I think he's just bad. But Lewis makes them all feel one of the family and gives them jobs to do to encourage them to be responsible. I expect we'll be murdered by one of them one of these days.' Gina laughed happily.

Miss Marple did not laugh.

They turned through some large gates where a man was standing on duty and went up a drive with bushes on both sides. The drive and gardens were not at all cared for.

Understanding Miss Marple's look, Gina said, 'It does look terrible. There were no gardeners during the war, and since then we haven't spent any money on it.'

They came round a curve and Stonygates appeared. It was huge – and as Gina had said, horrible.

'Ugly, isn't it?' said Gina affectionately. 'There's Grandma on the terrace. I'll stop here and you can go and meet her.'

★ ★ ★

Miss Marple walked along the terrace towards her old friend.

From a distance, the slim little figure looked girlish, even though she was leaning on a stick and moving slowly and painfully. It was as though a young girl was acting an old woman.

'Jane,' said Mrs Serrocold.

'Dear Carrie Louise.'

Yes, unmistakably Carrie Louise. Strangely unchanged still, although, unlike her sister, she used nothing artificial to make her look young. Her hair was grey, but it had always been silvery and had changed very little. Her skin was still pink and white, though now it was wrinkled. Her eyes still had their innocence. She had the slim figure of a girl and looked at the world with all the bright interest that her friend remembered.

'I do blame myself,' said Carrie Louise in her sweet voice, 'for letting it be so long. It has been years since I saw you, Jane dear. It's lovely that you've come here at last.'

From the end of the terrace Gina called, 'You ought to come in, Grandma. It's getting cold – and Jolly will be angry.'

Carrie Louise gave her little musical laugh. 'They all take care of me as if I was an old woman.'

'And you don't feel like one?'

'No, I don't, Jane. Even with all my pains, inside I still feel just like a young girl. Perhaps everyone does. It seems only a few months ago that we were in Florence. Do you remember Fraulein Schweich and her boots?'

The two women laughed together at events that had happened nearly half a century ago. They walked together to a side door where a very thin elderly lady met them. She had a proud nose, a short haircut and wore thick well-made clothes. She said fiercely, 'It's so bad of you, Carrie Louise, to stay out so late. You just do not take care of yourself. What will Mr Serrocold say?'

'Please don't be angry, Jolly,' said Carrie Louise.

She introduced Miss Marple. 'This is Miss Bellever, who is simply everything to me. Nurse, secretary, housekeeper and very faithful friend.'

Juliet 'Jolly' Bellever sniffed, and the end of her big nose turned rather pink, a sign of emotion. 'I do what I can,' she said in her deep voice. 'This is a very unorganized household. You simply cannot arrange any kind of routine.'

'Darling Jolly, where are you putting Miss Marple?'

'In the Blue Room. Shall I take her up?' asked Miss Bellever.

'Yes, please do, Jolly. And then bring her down to tea in the Hall.'

The Blue Room had heavy curtains of a rich blue that must have been, Miss Marple thought, fifty years old. The furniture was big and solid. Miss Bellever opened a door into a bathroom. This was unexpectedly modern.

'John Restarick had ten bathrooms put into the house,' Miss Bellever explained. 'That's about the only thing that's ever been modernized. Do you want a wash before tea?'

★ ★ ★

Miss Bellever took Miss Marple down the big grim staircase and across a huge dark hall and into a room where bookshelves went up to the ceiling and a big window looked out over a lake.

Carrie Louise was standing by the window and Miss Marple joined her.

'What a large house this is,' said Miss Marple. 'I feel quite lost in it.'

'Yes, there were fourteen living rooms – all huge. What can people do with more than one living room? And all those huge bedrooms – so much unnecessary space.'

'You haven't had it modernized?'

Carrie Louise looked surprised. 'No. Those things don't matter, do they? There are so many things that are much more important. We've just kept the Great Hall and the nearest rooms. But the East and West wings have been divided up, so that we have offices and bedrooms for the teaching staff. The boys are all in the College building – you can see it from here.'

Miss Marple looked out to where large red brick buildings showed through some trees. Then her eyes fell on something nearer, and she smiled. 'What a beautiful girl Gina is,' she said.

Carrie Louise's face lit up. 'Yes, isn't she?' she said softly. 'It's so lovely to have her back here again. I sent her to America at the beginning of the war – to Ruth. Poor Ruth! She was so upset about Gina's marriage. But I don't blame her. Ruth doesn't realize, as I do, that the old class differences are gone – or are going. Gina was doing her war work – and she met this young man, Walter Hudd. He was a Marine and had a very good war record. And a week later they were married. It was all far too quick, of course – there was no time to find out if they were really suited to each other – but that's the way of things nowadays. We may think young people are unwise, but we have to accept their decisions. Ruth, though, was terribly upset.'

'She didn't think the young man was suitable?'

'He came from the Midwest of America and had no money and no profession. He wasn't Ruth's idea of what was right for Gina. However, the thing was done. I was so pleased when they accepted my invitation to come over here. There's so much going on here – jobs of every kind. If Walter wants to make a start in medicine or get a degree or anything, he could do it in this country. After all, this is Gina's home. It's delightful to have her back.'

Miss Marple nodded and looked out of the window again at the two young people standing near the lake. 'They're a very handsome couple, too,' she said. 'I'm not surprised Gina fell in love with him!'

'Oh, but that isn't Walter. That's Steve – the younger of Johnnie Restarick's two boys. Steve is in charge of our Drama now. We have a theatre, you know, and plays – we encourage all the arts. Lewis says that so much of this juvenile crime is due to <u>showing-off</u>; most of the boys have had such an unhappy home life that their crimes make them feel like heroes. We encourage them to write their own plays and act in them and design and paint their own scenery. Steve is in charge of the theatre. It's wonderful, he's so enthusiastic.'

'I see,' said Miss Marple.

She did see very clearly the handsome face of Stephen Restarick as he stood talking eagerly to Gina. Gina's face she could not see, but there was no mistaking Stephen's expression. 'I suppose you realize, Carrie Louise,' said Miss Marple, 'that he's in love with her.'

'Oh no –' Carrie Louise looked troubled. 'I do hope not.'

Plan of Stonygates

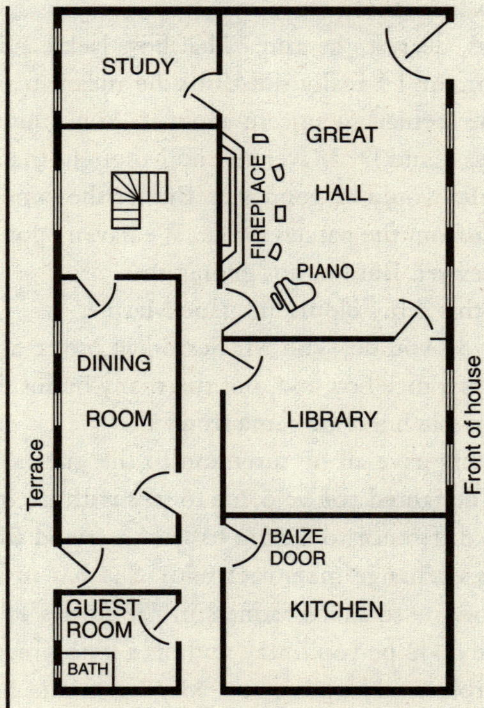

Chapter 4

Before Mrs Serrocold could say anything more, her husband came in from the hall carrying some letters.

Lewis Serrocold was a short man, but he had a strong personality. He was full of energy and he concentrated completely on who he was speaking to.

'Bad news, dearest,' he said. 'That boy, Jackie Flint. He's in trouble again. And I really did think he meant to stay honest this time. He seemed so sincere about it. You know he always liked railways – and Dr Maverick and I thought that if he got a railways job he would be good at it. But it's the same story. He's been stealing from the parcels office. We haven't got the answer to his troubles yet. But I'm not giving up.'

'Lewis – this is my old friend, Jane Marple.'

'Oh how do you do,' said Mr Serrocold, not really noticing Jane. 'Jackie is a nice boy, too, not too many brains, but a really nice boy. Terrible home he came from. I – '

He suddenly gave all his attention to the guest. 'Why, Miss Marple, I'm delighted you've come to stay with us. It will make such a great difference to Carrie to have a friend from the old days she can exchange memories with. She has in many ways a bad time here – so much sadness in the stories of these poor children. We do hope you'll stay with us a long time.'

Miss Marple could understand why her friend had been so attracted to this charming man. Though she was sure that Lewis Serrocold would always think that causes were more important than people. It might have made some women angry, but not Carrie Louise.

Lewis Serrocold took out another letter. 'And we do have some good news. This is from the bank. Young Morris is doing extremely well. They're very satisfied with him and are promoting him. I knew that all he needed was responsibility – that, and a thorough training in dealing with money.'

He turned to Miss Marple. 'Half these boys don't know what money is. It means no more to them than buying cigarettes – yet they're clever with numbers and find it exciting to use them. Well, I believe in training them – in accountancy – to show them how money works. Give them skill and then responsibility. Our greatest successes have been that way – only two out of thirty-eight have failed us. One is a head cashier – a really responsible position.' He broke off to say, 'Tea's all ready in the Hall, dearest,' to his wife.

Carrie Louise linked her arm through Miss Marple's and they went into the Great Hall. Tea seemed rather strange in these surroundings. The tea things were in a pile on a tray – inexpensive white cups mixed with the remains of some very good quality old tea services. There was a loaf of bread, two pots of jam, and some cheap-looking cakes.

A plump middle-aged woman with grey hair sat behind the tea table and Mrs Serrocold said, 'Jane, this is my daughter Mildred. You haven't seen her since she was a tiny girl.'

Mildred Strete looked exactly like a Canon's widow, wealthy, respectable and slightly boring. She was a plain woman with a large face. She had been, Miss Marple remembered, a very plain little girl.

'And this is Walter Hudd – Gina's husband.'

Walter was a big young man with hair brushed up on his head and a bad-tempered expression. He nodded uncomfortably and continued putting cake into his mouth.

Soon after, Gina came in with Stephen Restarick. They were both excited.

'Gina's got a wonderful idea for that scenery' said Stephen. 'You know, Gina, you've got a talent for theatrical designing.'

Gina laughed and looked pleased. Edgar Lawson came in and sat down by Lewis Serrocold. When Gina spoke to him, he did not answer.

★ ★ ★

There were more people at dinner, a young Dr Maverick, who was a psychiatrist, and whose detailed medical conversation was not easy to understand. There were also two young teachers, and a Mr Baumgarten, who was an occupational therapist, and three very shy young men. When there were guests, a few boys were chosen to learn how to behave properly at the dinner table. One of them, a fair-haired boy with blue eyes, was, Gina whispered to her, the expert at knocking people out.

The meal was badly cooked and badly served.

After dinner Lewis Serrocold went away with Dr Maverick to his office. The therapist and the teachers went away to their own rooms. The three 'juvenile <u>cases</u>' went back to the college. Gina and Stephen went to the college theatre. Mildred <u>knitted</u> and Miss Bellever repaired socks. Walter sat and stared at nothing. Carrie Louise and Miss Marple talked about the old days.

Edgar Lawson seemed unable to stay still. He sat down and then got up.

'I wonder if I ought to go to Mr Serrocold,' he said rather loudly. 'He may need me.'

Carrie Louise said gently, 'I don't think so. He was going to talk over some cases with Dr Maverick.'

'Then I certainly won't interrupt! I won't go where I'm not wanted. I've already wasted time today going down to the station when Mrs Hudd meant to go there herself.'

'Gina should have told you,' said Carrie Louise. 'But I think she just decided at the last moment.'

'You do understand, Mrs Serrocold, that she made me look a complete fool!'

'No, no,' said Carrie Louise, smiling. 'You mustn't have these ideas.'

'I know I'm not needed or wanted. I'm perfectly aware of that. If I had my proper place in life, things would be very different indeed. It's no fault of mine that I haven't got my proper place in life.'

'Now, Edgar,' said Carrie Louise. 'Don't get excited about nothing. Jane thinks it was very kind of you to meet her. Gina has these sudden ideas – she didn't mean to upset you.'

'Oh yes, she did. It was done on purpose – to make a fool of me.'

'Oh, Edgar.'

'You don't know half of what's going on, Mrs Serrocold. Well, I won't say any more now except goodnight.'

Edgar went out, shutting the door loudly.

Miss Bellever sniffed. 'Terrible manners.'

'He's so sensitive,' said Carrie Louise.

Mildred Strete said sharply, 'He is a horrible young man, Mother.'

'Lewis says he can't help it.'

Walter Hudd spoke for the first time that evening. 'That guy's crazy. That's all there is to it! Crazy!'

Chapter 5

The next morning, Miss Marple went out into the gardens. They were in a very bad way, the grass was long, the flower borders were full of weeds and the paths were overgrown. The kitchen gardens, on the other hand, were full of vegetables. And a large part of what had once been lawn and flower garden, was now tennis courts and a bowling green.

As Miss Marple pulled up a weed, Edgar Lawson appeared in a neat dark suit. She called him, asking if he knew where any gardening tools were kept. 'It's such a pity to see this,' said Miss Marple. 'I do like gardens. Now I don't suppose you ever think about gardens, Mr Lawson. You have so much important work to do for Mr Serrocold. You must find it all most interesting.'

He answered quickly, 'Yes – yes – it is interesting.'

'And you must be of the greatest help to Mr Serrocold.'

His face became troubled. 'I don't know. I can't be sure . . .' He broke off.

There was a garden seat nearby and Miss Marple sat down. 'I am sure,' she said brightly, 'that Mr Serrocold relies on you.'

'I don't know,' said Edgar. 'I really don't.' He sat down beside her. 'I'm in a very difficult position.'

'Of course,' said Miss Marple.

'This is all highly confidential,' he said.

'Of course,' said Miss Marple.

'Actually, my father is a very important man. Nobody knows except Mr Serrocold. You see, it might do my father's position harm if the story got out.' He smiled. A sad, dignified smile. 'You see, I'm Winston Churchill's son.'

'Oh,' said Miss Marple. 'I see.' And she did see. She remembered a rather sad story in St Mary Mead – and what had happened afterwards.

Edgar Lawson continued and what he said seemed more like a young man acting on a stage than talking about his life. 'There were reasons. My mother wasn't free. Her own husband was in a mental hospital – there could be no divorce – so there was no question of marriage. I don't really blame them. My father has always done everything he could – privately, of course. But the trouble is, he's got enemies – and they're against me, too. They keep us apart. They watch me. Wherever I go, they spy on me. And they make things go wrong for me.'

Miss Marple shook her head. 'Dear, dear,' she said.

'In London I was studying to be a doctor. They changed my exam answers. They wanted me to fail. They followed me, told things about me to my landlady. They follow me wherever I go. Mr Serrocold brought me down here. He was very kind. But even here, you know, I'm not safe. They're here, too – working against me – making the others dislike me. Mr Serrocold says that isn't true – but Mr Serrocold doesn't know. Or else – I wonder – sometimes I've thought . . .' He got up. 'This is all confidential. You do understand that, don't you? But if you notice anyone following me – spying, I mean – let me know who it is!'

He went away, and Miss Marple watched him and wondered. There was something a little wrong about Edgar Lawson – perhaps more than a little. And Edgar Lawson reminded her of someone.

A voice spoke. 'Crazy. Just crazy.'

Walter Hudd was standing beside her. He was frowning as he stared after Edgar. 'What kind of a place is this, anyway?' he said. 'They're all crazy. That Edgar guy – what do you think about him? He says his father's really General Montgomery. He told Gina he was the heir to the Russian throne. Hell, doesn't the guy know who his father really was?'

'I should imagine not,' said Miss Marple. 'That is probably the trouble.'

Walter sat down beside her. 'They're all crazy here.'

'You don't like Stonygates?'

The young man frowned. 'I simply don't understand! They're rich, these people. And look at the way they live. Old broken cups and plates and cheap stuff all mixed up. No proper servants. Curtains and chair covers falling to pieces! Mrs Serrocold just doesn't care. Look at that dress she was wearing last night. Nearly worn out – and yet she can buy what she likes. Money? They're so rich.'

He paused, thinking. 'There's nothing wrong with being poor, if you're young and strong and ready to work. I had some money saved. Gina comes from a better family than me. But it didn't matter. We fell in love – we are mad about each other. We got married. We were going to open a garage back home – Gina was willing. Then that arrogant Aunt Ruth of Gina's started making trouble and Gina wanted to come here to England to see her grandmother. Well, that seemed fair enough. It was her home, and I wanted to see England anyway. So we came. Just a visit – that's what I thought.'

He became more angry, 'But we got caught up in this crazy business. Why don't we stay here – that's what they say? Plenty of jobs for me. Jobs? I don't want a job feeding sweets to baby criminals! Don't people who've got money understand their luck? Don't they understand that most of the world can't have a great place like this? Isn't it crazy to turn your back on your luck when you've got it? I'll work the way I like and at what I like. This place makes me feel I'm trapped. And Gina – I don't understand her anymore. I can't even talk to her now. Oh hell!'

Miss Marple said gently, 'I quite see your point of view.'

Walter gave her a look. 'You're the only one I've talked to so far. I don't know what it is about you – I know you're English – but you do remind me of my Aunt Betsy back home.'

'Now that's very nice.'

'She had a lot of sense,' Walter continued thoughtfully. 'She looked weak, but she was tough – yes, ma'am, I'll say she was tough.'

He got up. 'Sorry about talking to you in this way.' For the first time, Miss Marple saw him smile. It was a very attractive smile, and Walter Hudd was suddenly changed from an awkward bad-tempered boy into a handsome and charming young man. 'I had to say it, I suppose. But I wasn't right to worry you.'

'Not at all, my dear boy,' said Miss Marple. 'I have a nephew of my own.'

'You've got other company coming,' said Walter Hudd. 'That woman doesn't like me. Goodbye, ma'am. Thanks for the talk.' He walked away and Miss Marple watched Mildred Strete coming across the lawn to join her.

* * *

'I see you've been bothered by that terrible young man,' said Mrs Strete, as she sat down. 'What a tragedy that is.'

'A tragedy?'

'Gina's marriage. I told Mother it was unwise to send her off to America.'

'It must have been difficult to decide what was right,' said Miss Marple. 'Where children were concerned, I mean. With the possibility of a German invasion.'

'Nonsense,' said Mrs Strete. 'I knew we would win the war. But Mother has always been unreasonable where Gina is concerned. The child was always spoilt. Oh you've no idea, Aunt Jane,' she cried suddenly, 'And then there's Mother's idealistic projects. This whole place is impossible. Lewis thinks of nothing but these horrible young criminals. And Mother thinks of nothing but him. Everything Lewis does is right. Look at the garden and the house – nothing is done properly. There's more than enough money. It's just that nobody cares. Mother won't even buy herself proper clothes. If it were my house . . .' She stopped and then said in surprise, 'Here is Lewis. How strange. He rarely comes into the garden.'

Mr Serrocold came towards them in the same single-minded way that he did everything. He appeared not to notice Mildred because it was only Miss Marple who was in his mind.

'I'm so sorry,' he said. 'I wanted to take you round and show you everything. But I must go to Liverpool to help Jackie Flint. If only we can get the police not to prosecute.'

Mildred Strete got up and walked away. Lewis Serrocold did not notice. His earnest eyes looked at Miss Marple through thick glasses. 'You see,' he said, 'the police nearly always take the wrong view. Prison is no good at all. Corrective training like we have here . . .'

Miss Marple interrupted him. 'Mr Serrocold,' she said. 'Are you satisfied that young Mr Lawson is – is quite normal?'

A worried expression appeared on Lewis Serrocold's face. 'I do hope he's not getting worse again. What has he been saying?'

'He told me that he was Winston Churchill's son.'

'Of course – of course. The usual statements. He's illegitimate, as you've probably guessed, poor boy, and from a very poor family. He hit a man in the street who he said was spying on him. It was all very typical. His father was a sailor – the mother didn't even know his name. The child started imagining things about his father and about himself. He wore uniform and medals that he had no right to wear – all very typical. But Doctor Maverick believes we can help give him self-confidence, make him understand that it's not a man's family background that is important, but what he is. There has been a great improvement. And now you say . . .' He shook his head.

'Could he be dangerous, Mr Serrocold? He talked to me of enemies – of persecution. Isn't that a dangerous sign?'

'I don't think so. But I'll speak to Maverick. So far, he has been very hopeful.'

He looked at his watch. 'I must go. Ah, here is our dear Jolly. She will look after you.'

Miss Bellever arrived in a hurry. 'The car is at the door, Mr Serrocold. I will take Miss Marple over to Dr Maverick at the Institute.'

'Thank you. I must go.' Lewis Serrocold hurried away.

Looking after him, Miss Bellever said, 'Some day that man will simply fall down dead. He never rests.'

'He is passionate about this cause,' said Miss Marple.

'He never thinks of anything else,' said Miss Bellever grimly. 'His wife is a sweet woman, as you know, Miss Marple, and she should have love and attention. But the only thing people here think about is a lot of dishonest boys who don't want to do any hard work. What about the good boys from good homes? Why isn't something done for them? Honesty just isn't interesting to cranks like Mr Serrocold and Dr Maverick.'

They crossed the garden and came to the grand gate, which Eric Gulbrandsen had built as an entrance to his ugly, red brick college building.

Dr Maverick, looking, Miss Marple decided, not normal himself, came out to meet them. 'Thank you, Miss Bellever,' he said. 'Now, Miss Marple, in our view, psychiatry is the answer.

It's a medical problem – that's what we've got to get the police and the law courts to understand. Do look up, you'll see how we begin.'

Miss Marple looked up over the doorway and read:

RECOVER HOPE ALL YOU WHO ENTER HERE

'Isn't that just right! We don't want to punish these boys. We want to make them feel what fine young men they are.'

'Like Edgar Lawson?' said Miss Marple.

'Interesting case, that. Have you been talking to him?'

'He has been talking to me,' said Miss Marple. 'I wondered if, perhaps, he isn't a little mad?'

Dr Maverick laughed cheerfully. 'We're all mad, dear lady,' he hurried her in through the door. 'That's the secret. We're all a little mad.'

Chapter 6

On the whole it was rather an exhausting day.

Enthusiasm can be extremely tiring, Miss Marple thought. She felt dissatisfied with herself. There was a pattern here – perhaps several patterns – and yet she could not get a clear view of them. Any worry she felt was centred round Edgar Lawson.

Something was wrong about Edgar Lawson – something that went beyond the admitted facts. But Miss Marple could not see how that wrongness, whatever it was, affected her friend Carrie Louise.

When, on the following morning Carrie Louise came and sat down on the garden seat beside her and asked her what she was thinking about, Miss Marple replied, '*You*, Carrie Louise.'

'What about me?'

'Tell me honestly – is there anything here that worries you?'

'Worries me?' The woman raised clear blue eyes. 'But Jane, what should worry me?'

'Well, most of us have worries.' Miss Marple's eyes were bright. 'I worry about things eating the vegetables I grow in my garden – getting sheets properly repaired. Oh, lots of little things – it seems unnatural that you shouldn't have any worries at all.'

'I suppose I must have,' said Mrs Serrocold. 'Lewis works too hard, and Stephen forgets his meals, working so hard at the theatre, and Gina is very nervous – but I've never been able to change people – I don't see how you can. So it wouldn't be any good worrying, would it?'

'Mildred's not very happy, either, is she?'

'Oh no,' said Carrie Louise. 'Mildred is never happy. She wasn't as a child. Quite unlike Pippa.'

'Perhaps,' suggested Miss Marple, 'there was a reason for Mildred not to be happy?'

Carrie Louise said quietly, 'Because of being jealous? Yes, I suppose that could be true. But people don't really need a cause for feeling what they feel. They're just made that way. Don't you think so, Jane?'

Miss Marple said, 'I expect you're right, Carrie Louise.'

'Of course, not having any worries is partly because of Jolly. Dear Jolly. She takes care of me as though I were a baby. She would do anything for me. I really believe Jolly would murder someone for me, Jane. Isn't that a terrible thing to say?'

'She's certainly devoted,' agreed Miss Marple.

'She would like me to buy wonderful clothes and every luxury, and she thinks everybody ought to take care of me,' Mrs Serrocold's musical laugh rang out. 'All our poor boys are, in her view, spoilt young criminals and not worth the trouble. She thinks this place is bad for my arthritis, and I ought to go somewhere warm and dry.'

'Do you suffer much from arthritis?'

'It's got much worse lately. I find it difficult to walk – I get awful pains in my legs. Oh well –' again there came that lovely smile, 'these things come with age.'

Miss Bellever came out of the French windows and hurried across to them. 'A telegram has just come. *Arriving this afternoon, Christian Gulbrandsen.*'

'Christian?' Carrie Louise looked surprised. 'I had no idea he was in England.'

'Shall I put him in the guest room?'

'Yes, please, Jolly. Then there will be no stairs.'

Miss Bellever returned to the house.

'Christian Gulbrandsen is my stepson,' said Carrie Louise. 'My first husband's eldest son. Actually he's two years older than

I am. He's the main trustee of the Institute. How very annoying that Lewis is away.'

Christian Gulbrandsen arrived that afternoon in time for tea. He was a big heavy-featured man, with a slow way of talking. He greeted Carrie Louise with every sign of affection. 'And how is our little Carrie Louise? You don't look a day older.' His hands on her shoulders, he stood smiling down at her.

A hand pulled his sleeve. 'Christian!'

'Ah,' he turned – 'it is Mildred? How are you, Mildred?'

Christian Gulbrandsen and his half-sister looked very much alike – though there was nearly thirty years' difference in age. Mildred seemed particularly pleased by his arrival.

'And how is little Gina?' said Gulbrandsen, turning to her. 'You and your husband are still here, then?'

'Yes. We've quite settled down, haven't we, Walter?'

'It looks like it,' said Walter, unfriendly as usual.

'So here I am with all the family again,' said Gulbrandsen. He spoke with a determined happiness – but in fact, Miss Marple thought, he was not happy. There was a grim look about him.

Introduced to Miss Marple, he looked at her with careful attention.

'We had no idea you were in England, Christian,' said Mrs Serrocold. 'It is too bad that Lewis is away.'

'It is necessary that I see Lewis. When will he be back?'

'Tomorrow afternoon. If only you had let us know.'

'My dear Carrie Louise, my arrangements were made very suddenly.'

Miss Bellever said to Miss Marple, 'Mr Gulbrandsen and Mr Serrocold are trustees of the Gulbrandsen Institute. The others are the Bishop of Cromer and Mr Gilfoy.'

It appeared, then, that it was business that brought Christian Gulbrandsen to Stonygates. It seemed to be what everyone else thought. And yet Miss Marple wondered.

Once or twice the old man looked at Carrie Louise in a way that puzzled Miss Marple. Then he moved his eyes to the others, making a sort of hidden judgement.

After tea, Miss Marple tactfully left the family and went into the library. Rather to her surprise, when she had settled herself with her knitting, Christian Gulbrandsen came in and sat down beside her.

'You are a very old friend, I think, of our dear Carrie Louise?' he said.

'We were at school together in Italy, Mr Gulbrandsen. Many years ago.'

'Ah yes. And you are fond of her?'

'Yes, indeed,' said Miss Marple warmly.

'So, I think, is everyone. And it should be so, for she is a very dear and lovely person. I and my brothers have always loved her. She has been like a very dear sister. She was loyal to my father and to all his ideas. She has never thought of herself, but put the needs of others first.'

'She has always been an idealist,' said Miss Marple.

'An idealist? Yes. Yes, that is so. And therefore it may be that she does not truly understand the evil that there is in the world.'

Miss Marple looked at him, surprised.

'Tell me,' he said. 'How is her health?'

Again Miss Marple felt surprised. 'She seems to me very well – apart from arthritis.'

'Arthritis? Yes. And her heart? Her heart is good?'

'As far as I know. But until yesterday I had not seen her for many years. If you want to know the state of her health, you should ask somebody in the house here. Miss Bellever, for instance.'

Christian Gulbrandsen was staring at her very hard. 'Sometimes,' he said simply, 'it is hard to know what is the best thing to do. I wish to act for the best. I am particularly anxious that no harm and no unhappiness should come to that dear lady. But it is not easy – not easy at all.'

Mrs Strete came into the room at that moment. 'Christian, Dr Maverick wants to know if you would like to discuss anything with him.'

'No, I will wait until Lewis returns. But I will have a word with him.'

Gulbrandsen hurried out. Mildred Strete stared after him and then stared at Miss Marple. 'I wonder if anything is wrong. Christian is very unlike himself. Did he say anything?'

'He only asked me about your mother's health.'

'Her health? Why would he ask you about that?' Mildred spoke sharply, her large square face went red.

'I really don't know.'

'Mother's health is perfectly good. Surprising for a woman of her age. I hope you told him so?'

'I don't really know anything about it,' said Miss Marple. 'He asked me about her heart.'

'There's nothing wrong with Mother's heart!'

'I'm delighted to hear you say so, my dear.'

'What on earth put all these strange ideas into Christian's head?'

'I've no idea,' said Miss Marple.

Chapter 7

The next day seemed uneventful.

Christian Gulbrandsen spent the morning with Dr Maverick in the Institute. In the early afternoon Gina took him for a drive, and after that he asked Miss Bellever to show him the gardens. It seemed to Miss Marple that he wanted a private talk with her.

The only disturbing thing happened about four o'clock. Miss Marple had gone out in the garden to take a walk before tea. Coming round some overgrown bushes she met Edgar Lawson, who was rushing along, talking to himself and who nearly ran into her.

He said, 'I beg your pardon,' but Miss Marple was startled by the strange staring expression of his eyes. 'Aren't you feeling well, Mr Lawson?'

'Well? I've had a shock – a terrible shock.' The young man gave a quick look past her, and then an uneasy look to either side. 'Shall I tell you?' He looked at her doubtfully. 'I don't know. I don't really know. I've been spied on so much.'

Miss Marple took him firmly by the arm. 'If we walk down this path – there, now, there are no trees or bushes near. Nobody can overhear.'

'No – no, you're right.' He took a deep breath, bent his head and almost whispered, 'I've made a terrible discovery.' Edgar Lawson began to shake. He was almost crying. 'I trusted someone! I believed them, but it was lies – all lies. Lies to keep me from finding out the truth. It's so cruel. You see, he was the one person I trusted, and now to find out that all the time he's been my enemy! It's he who put spies to watch me. But he can't get away with it any more. I shall speak out. I shall tell him I know what he has been doing.'

'Who is "he"?' demanded Miss Marple.

Edgar Lawson stood up straight. 'My father.'

'Montgomery – or do you mean Winston Churchill?'

Edgar gave her a disapproving look. 'They let me think that – just to keep me from learning the truth. But I know now. I've got a friend – a real friend who tells me the truth. Well, my father will have to face me. I'll throw his lies in his face! We'll see what he's got to say to that.' And suddenly Edgar ran off.

Her face serious, Miss Marple went back to the house.

'We're all a little mad,' Dr Maverick had said.

But it seemed to her that in Edgar's case it went further than that.

⋆⋆⋆

Lewis Serrocold arrived back at six-thirty. He stopped the car at the gates and walked to the house through the gardens. From her window, Miss Marple saw Christian Gulbrandsen go out to meet him and the two men turned to walk along the terrace and back.

Miss Marple had been careful to bring her bird-watching binoculars with her. She noticed, before lifting the binoculars to her eyes, that both men were looking very worried. Miss Marple leant out a little farther. Bits of conversation reached her now and then. If the men looked up, it would be obvious that an enthusiastic bird watcher had her attention fixed far away from their conversation.

'. . . how to save Carrie Louise from knowing . . .' Gulbrandsen was saying.

The next time they passed below, Lewis Serrocold was speaking, '. . . if it can be kept from her. I agree that we must consider her . . .'

Other faint words came to the listener.

'. . . really serious . . .'

'. . . too big a responsibility to take . . .'

'. . . we should take outside advice . . .'

Finally Miss Marple heard Christian Gulbrandsen say, 'It is getting cold. We must go inside.'

Miss Marple drew her head in through the window. Whatever was wrong at Stonygates, it definitely affected Carrie Louise.

★ ★ ★

Dinner that evening was very quiet. Both Gulbrandsen and Lewis were deep in their own thoughts. When they moved into the Hall afterwards, Christian said he had an important letter to write. 'So if you will forgive me, dear Carrie Louise, I will go to my room.'

He left the Great Hall by the door which led past the main staircase and along a corridor, at the end of which was the guest room and bathroom.

When he had gone Carrie Louise said, 'Aren't you going down to the theatre tonight, Gina?'

The girl shook her head. She went over and sat by the window overlooking the front drive.

Stephen sat down at the grand piano and started playing very quietly – a sad little tune. The teachers and Dr Maverick said goodnight and left. As Walter turned on a reading lamp, there was a loud bang and half the lights went out.

He growled. 'That damn switch is faulty. I'll go and put a new fuse in.'

He left the Hall and Carrie Louise said quietly, 'Walter's so clever with electrical things. You remember how he fixed that toaster?'

'Has mother taken her medicine?' Mildred asked.

Miss Bellever looked annoyed. 'I completely forgot.' She jumped up and went into the dining room, returning with a glass of rose-coloured medicine.

Carrie Louise held out her hand. 'It's such horrible stuff and nobody lets me forget it,' she said, making a face.

And then, unexpectedly, Lewis Serrocold said, 'I don't think you should take it tonight, my dear. I'm not sure it's really good for you.'

Quietly, but with that controlled energy always so obvious in him, he took the glass from Miss Bellever and put it down on the table.

'Really, Mr Serrocold,' Miss Bellever said, 'I can't agree with you. Mrs Serrocold has been very much better since . . .'

She broke off as the front door was pushed violently open with a bang. Edgar Lawson came into the big hall as if he were a star performer making a grand entry.

He stood in the middle of the floor and said dramatically, 'So I have found you, my enemy!'

He said it to Lewis Serrocold.

Mr Serrocold looked amazed. 'Why, Edgar, what is the matter?'

'You can say that to me – you! You who know! You've been lying to me, spying on me, working with my enemies against me.'

Lewis took him by the arm. 'Now, now, my dear boy, don't excite yourself. Tell me all about it quietly. Come into my study.'

He led him across the Hall and through a door on the right, closing it behind him. Then there was the sound of a key being turned in the lock.

Miss Bellever looked at Miss Marple, the same idea in both their minds. It was not Lewis Serrocold who had turned the key.

Miss Bellever said quickly, 'That young man is about to lose control of himself. It isn't safe.'

Mildred said, 'He's unbalanced – and ungrateful. You ought to have him locked up, Mother.'

With a sigh Carrie Louise said, 'There's no harm in him really. He's very fond of Lewis.'

Miss Marple looked at her curiously. There had been no fondness in Edgar's expression, very far from it.

Gina said sharply, 'Edgar was holding something in his pocket.'

Stephen stopped playing.

'I think you know,' Miss Marple said, 'it was a gun.'

From behind the door of Lewis's office the sound of voices was clear and loud. Edgar Lawson shouted while Lewis Serrocold's voice stayed calm.

'Lies, lies, all lies. You're my father. I'm your son. You've deprived me of my rights. I should own this place. You hate me – you want to get rid of me!'

There was a calming sound from Lewis and then the hysterical voice screamed out horrible swear words. Edgar seemed to be losing control of himself. Occasional words came from Lewis, 'Calm – just be calm – you know none of this is true.' But they seemed to anger the young man further.

Everyone in the Hall was silent, listening to what was happening behind the locked door of Lewis's study.

'I'll make you listen to me,' yelled Edgar. 'I'll take that superior expression off your face. I'll have revenge for all you've made me suffer.'

The other voice said sharply, 'Put that gun down!'

Gina cried, 'Edgar will kill him. He's mad. Can't we get the police?'

Carrie Louise, still unmoved, said softly, 'There's no need to worry, Gina. Edgar loves Lewis. He's just being dramatic, that's all.'

Edgar laughed then, in a way that sounded mad to Miss Marple. 'Yes, I've got a gun. You started this conspiracy against me and now you're going to pay for it.'

What sounded like a gun firing made them all jump, but Carrie Louise said, 'It's all right, it's outside – in the park somewhere.'

Edgar was screaming. 'Why don't you get down on your knees and beg for your life? I'm going to shoot, I tell you. I'm going to shoot you dead! I'm your son – your unacknowledged hated son – you wanted me hidden away, out of the world altogether, perhaps. You set your spies to follow me – you conspired against me. You, my father! My father. You went on telling me lies. Pretending to be kind to me, and all the time – all the time – You're not fit to live. I won't let you live.'

Again Edgar began screaming horrible swear words. At some point during the scene Miss Marple was conscious of Miss Bellever saying, 'We must do something,' and leaving the Hall.

Edgar seemed to pause for breath and then he shouted out, 'You're going to die – to die. You're going to die now. Take that, you devil, and that!'

Two shots rang out – not in the park this time, but definitely behind the locked door.

Mildred, cried out, 'Oh no, what shall we do?'

There was a loud noise from inside the room and then the sound of slow, heavy sobbing.

Stephen Restarick marched past Miss Marple and started knocking loudly on the door. 'Open the door. Open the door,' he shouted.

Miss Bellever came back into the Hall, holding several keys. 'Try these,' she said breathlessly.

At that moment the lights came on again. Stephen Restarick began trying the keys. They heard the inside key fall out as he did so.

And that wild, desperate sobbing went on.

Walter Hudd, coming lazily back into the Hall, stopped and demanded, 'What's going on?'

Mildred said tearfully, 'That awful mad young man has shot Mr Serrocold.'

'Please.' It was Carrie Louise who spoke. She got up and came across to the study door. Gently she pushed Stephen Restarick aside. 'Let me speak to him.'

She called – very softly – 'Edgar, Edgar, let me in, will you? Please, Edgar.'

They heard the key put into the lock. It turned and the door was opened.

But it was not Edgar who opened it. It was Lewis Serrocold. He was breathing hard as though he had been running – otherwise he was not affected.

'It's all right, dearest,' he said. 'It's all right.'

'We thought you had been shot,' said Miss Bellever, her relief obvious.

Lewis Serrocold frowned. He said with a little show of anger, 'Of course I haven't been shot.'

They could see into the study by now. Edgar Lawson had fallen by the desk. He was sobbing and breathing heavily. The gun lay on the floor.

'But we heard the shots,' said Mildred.

'Oh yes, he fired twice.'

'And he missed you?'

'Of course he missed me,' snapped Lewis.

No, no, Miss Marple did not consider those were the right words at all. The shots must have been fired at close range.

Lewis Serrocold said irritably, 'Where's Maverick? It's Maverick we need.'

Miss Bellever said, 'I'll get him. Shall I call the police as well?'

'Police? Certainly not.'

'Of course we must call the police,' said Mildred. 'He's dangerous.'

'Nonsense,' said Lewis Serrocold. 'Poor boy. Does he look dangerous?'

At that moment he looked young and helpless. His voice had lost its careful accent. 'I didn't mean to do it,' he groaned. 'I don't know what happened to me – saying all that stuff – I must have been mad. I didn't mean to. Please, Mr Serrocold, I really didn't mean to.'

Lewis Serrocold patted him on the shoulder. 'That's all right, my boy. No damage done.'

'I might have killed you, Mr Serrocold.'

Walter Hudd walked across the room and looked at the wall behind the desk.

'The bullets went in here. It must have been a near miss,' he said grimly.

'I didn't know what I was doing. I thought he'd taken away my rights. I thought . . .'

Miss Marple asked the question she had been wanting to ask for some time. 'Who told you that Mr Serrocold was your father?'

Just for a second a sly expression showed on Edgar's pain-filled face. It was there and gone in a second. 'Nobody,' he said. 'I just – I just thought it.'

Walter Hudd picked up the gun. 'Where the hell did you get my gun?' he demanded. 'You little thief, you took it out of my room!'

Lewis Serrocold stepped between the frightened Edgar and the angry American. 'Ah, here's Maverick. Take a look at him, will you?'

Dr Maverick came towards Edgar enthusiastically. 'This is not acceptable, Edgar. You can't do this sort of thing, you know.'

'He's mad and dangerous,' said Mildred. 'He's been shooting a gun at my stepfather.'

Edgar cried out in fear.

'Careful, please, Mrs Strete,' Dr Maverick warned.

'I'm sick of you all! I tell you this man's mad,' Mildred insisted.

Edgar pulled away from Dr Maverick and fell to the floor at Serrocold's feet. 'Help me. Help me. Don't let them take me away and lock me up. Don't let them!'

'You come with me, Edgar,' said Dr Maverick. 'You go to bed now – and we'll talk in the morning. Now you trust me, don't you?'

Rising to his feet and shaking, Edgar looked doubtfully at the young doctor and then at Mildred Strete. 'She said – I was mad.'

'No, no, you're not.'

Miss Bellever came in, red faced. 'I've telephoned the police,' she said grimly.

'Jolly!' Carrie Louise cried in dismay.

Edgar began crying again.

'I told you, Jolly, I did not want the police,' Lewis Serrocold said angrily. 'This is a medical matter.'

'That may be so,' said Miss Bellever. 'But I had to call the police. Mr Gulbrandsen's been shot dead.'

Chapter 8

'Christian shot? Dead?' Carrie Louise said. 'That's impossible.'

'Go and look for yourselves,' said Miss Bellever angrily.

Lewis Serrocold put a hand on Carrie Louise's shoulder. 'No, dearest, let me go.'

He went out. Dr Maverick and Miss Bellever followed him.

Miss Marple gently led Carrie Louise to a chair. She sat down, her eyes looking hurt and shocked. 'Christian – shot?' she said again. She sounded like a hurt, confused child. 'But who could possibly want to shoot Christian?'

'Crazy!' Walter said quietly. 'The whole lot of them.'

Gina's young, startled face was the most vivid thing in the room.

Suddenly the front door opened and together with a rush of cold air a man in a big overcoat came in.

His cheerful greeting seemed shocking. 'Hello, everybody. A lot of fog on the road, I had to drive very slowly.'

Miss Marple saw that this must be the other Restarick brother, Alex, but where Stephen was thin, the newcomer was a much bigger young man, handsome and with the all the authority and good humour that success brings to some men.

He said, doubtfully, 'You were expecting me, weren't you? You got my telegram?'

He was speaking now to Carrie Louise. She put her hand out to him. He took it and kissed it gently with real affection.

'Alex dear – things have been happening.'

'My brother, Christian,' Mildred said with a grim relish that Miss Marple disliked, 'has been shot dead.'

'Good grief,' Alex said, clearly upset. 'Suicide, do you mean?'

'Oh no,' Carrie Louise said. 'It couldn't be suicide. Not Christian!'

'Uncle Christian would never shoot himself,' said Gina.

'When did this happen?' asked Alex.

'About – oh three or four minutes ago, I suppose,' said Gina. 'Why, of course, we heard the shot. Only we didn't notice it. You see, there were other things going on.'

Juliet Bellever came into the Hall. 'Mr Serrocold suggests that we all wait in the library for the police. Except for Mrs Serrocold. You've had a shock, Carrie. I'll take you up to bed.'

Rising, Carrie Louise shook her head. 'I must see Christian first.' She looked round. 'Come with me, will you, Jane?'

The two women moved out through the door, past the main staircase and the dining room, past the side door to the terrace and on to the guest room that had been given to Christian Gulbrandsen. It was furnished as a sitting room more than a bedroom, with a bed on one side and a door leading into a dressing room and bathroom.

Christian had been sitting at the desk with a typewriter in front of him. He sat there now, fallen sideways in the chair.

Lewis Serrocold was standing by the window looking out into the night.

He turned. 'My dearest, you shouldn't have come.'

'Oh yes, Lewis. I had to see him. One has to know how things are.'

She walked slowly towards the desk. 'He was shot deliberately by someone? Murdered?'

'Oh yes.'

She stood looking down at the dead man. There was sadness and affection in her face. 'Dear Christian,' she said. 'He was always good to me.' Softly, she touched the top of his head with her fingers. 'Bless you and thank you, dear Christian.'

Lewis Serrocold said with more emotion than Miss Marple had seen in him before, 'I wish I could have saved you from this.'

His wife shook her head gently. 'You can't really save anyone from anything,' she said. 'Things always have to be faced sooner or later. And therefore it had better be sooner.'

Chapter 9

Inspector Curry and his Sergeant found Miss Bellever alone in the Great Hall when they arrived.

She came forward. 'I am Juliet Bellever, companion and secretary to Mrs Serrocold. Most of the household are in the library. Mr Serrocold remained in Mr Gulbrandsen's room to see that nothing was touched. Dr Maverick, who first examined the body, will be here soon. He had to take a – case over to the Institute. Shall I lead the way?'

'Please.'

For the next twenty minutes it was the routine of police procedure that was most important. The photographer took pictures. The police surgeon arrived and was joined by Dr Maverick. Half an hour later, the ambulance took away Christian Gulbrandsen, and Inspector Curry started his official inquiry.

He looked carefully round the people gathered there, making notes in his mind. An old lady with white hair, a middle-aged lady, the good-looking girl he had seen driving her car round the countryside, that American husband of hers. A couple of young men, the capable Miss Bellever, and Lewis Serrocold.

'I'm afraid this is all very upsetting to you,' he said, 'and I hope I will not keep you too long this evening. We can look at everything more thoroughly tomorrow. It was Miss Bellever who found Mr Gulbrandsen dead, so I'll ask her to give me a description of the general situation. Mr Serrocold, if you want to go up to your wife, please do.'

* * *

Miss Bellever arranged Inspector Curry, his Sergeant and herself in Lewis Serrocold's study. Inspector Curry had a pleasant voice and manner. He looked quiet and serious. 'I've had the main facts from Mr Serrocold. Mr Christian Gulbrandsen was one of the trustees here and he arrived unexpectedly yesterday. That is correct?'

'Yes.'

Inspector Curry was pleased by her short answer. He continued, 'Mr Serrocold was away in Liverpool. He returned this evening by the 6.30 train.'

'Yes.'

'After dinner, Mr Gulbrandsen went to work in his own room, leaving the rest of the group here. Correct?'

'Yes.'

'Now, Miss Bellever, please explain how you found him dead.'

'Something unpleasant happened this evening. A young man became very unbalanced and threatened Mr Serrocold with a gun. They were locked in this room and you can see the bullet holes in the wall there. Fortunately Mr Serrocold was unhurt. After firing the shots, this young man was in such a bad condition that Mr Serrocold sent me to find Dr Maverick. As I was coming back, I went to Mr Gulbrandsen's room to ask if there was anything he would like before he went to bed. When I saw that Mr Gulbrandsen was dead, I rang you.'

'Could anyone have come into the house from outside without being heard or seen?'

'Certainly – by the side door to the terrace. People come in and out that way to go to the College buildings.'

'And you have, I believe, two hundred and fifty juvenile delinquents in the College?'

'Yes. But the College buildings are locked and guarded. It is most unlikely that anyone could leave the College without permission.'

'We shall check that, of course. What was the purpose of Mr Gulbrandsen's visit?'

'I have no idea. His business here was with Mr Serrocold.'

'Did he have a meeting with Mr Serrocold?'

'No, there was no time. Mr Serrocold arrived just before dinner. And after dinner, Mr Gulbrandsen said he had an important letter to write and went away to do so.'

'He didn't suggest a meeting with Mr Serrocold?'

'No.'

'Mr Serrocold did not go with him to his room?'

'No. Mr Serrocold stayed in the Hall.'

'And you have no idea at what time Mr Gulbrandsen was killed?'

'I think it is possible that we heard the shot. If so, it was at twenty-three minutes past nine. Naturally I looked at the clock.'

'You heard a shot? And it did not frighten you?'

'The circumstances were already very frightening.' Miss Bellever explained in more detail the scene between Lewis Serrocold and Edgar Lawson. Then added grimly, 'You don't expect murder and attempted murder in the same house on the same night.'

Inspector Curry agreed to the truth of that.

'All the same,' said Miss Bellever, suddenly, 'You know, I believe that's what made me go along to Mr Gulbrandsen's room later. To reassure myself that everything was all right.'

Inspector Curry stared at her for a moment. 'What made you think it might not be all right?'

'The shot outside. It didn't mean anything at the time. And afterwards I told myself that it was only a backfire from Mr Restarick's car. But . . .'

'Mr Restarick's car?'

'Yes. Alex Restarick arrived this evening – just after all this happened.'

'I see. When you discovered Mr Gulbrandsen's body, did you touch anything?'

'Of course not. Mr Gulbrandsen had been shot through the head but there was no gun to be seen, so I knew it was murder and not suicide.'

'And just now, when you took us into the room, everything was the same as when you found the body?'

Miss Bellever thought about it. 'One thing was different,' she said. 'There was nothing in the typewriter. Mr Gulbrandsen had been writing a letter, it must have been removed.'

'Thank you, Miss Bellever. Who else went into that room before we arrived?'

'Mr Serrocold, of course. And Mrs Serrocold and Miss Marple.'

'Which is Miss Marple?' Inspector Curry asked.

'The old lady with white hair. She was a school friend of Mrs Serrocold's. She arrived about four days ago.'

'Well, thank you, Miss Bellever. I'll have a word with Miss Marple next, then she can go off to bed. It's not kind to keep an old lady like that from her rest,' said Inspector Curry. 'This must have been a shock to her.'

'I'll tell her, shall I?'

'Yes, please do.'

Miss Bellever went out. Inspector Curry looked at the ceiling. 'Why Gulbrandsen?' he said. 'Two hundred and fifty young delinquents here. Probably one of them did it. But why Gulbrandsen? The stranger.'

Sergeant Lake said, 'Of course we don't know everything yet.'

Inspector Curry said, 'So far, we don't know anything at all.'

He jumped up when Miss Marple came in and hurried to make her feel comfortable. 'Now don't upset yourself, ma'am. This is all very worrying, I know. But we've just got to get the facts clear.'

'Oh yes, I know,' said Miss Marple. 'So difficult, isn't it? To be clear about anything, I mean. Because if you're looking at one thing, you can't be looking at another. And one so often looks at the wrong thing, though whether because one happens to do so or because you're meant to, it's very hard to say. Misdirection, the magicians call it. So clever, aren't they?'

Inspector Curry blinked a little. 'Quite so. Now, ma'am, Miss Bellever has told me what happened this evening. A most anxious time for all of you, I'm sure.'

'Yes, indeed. It was all so dramatic, you know.'

'First, this argument between Mr Serrocold and Edgar Lawson.'

'A very strange young man,' said Miss Marple. 'I have felt all along that there was something wrong about him.'

'I'm sure you have,' said Inspector Curry. 'And then, after that excitement was over, there came Mr Gulbrandsen's death. I understand that you went with Mrs Serrocold to see the – er – the body.'

'Yes, I did. We are very old friends.'

'Quite so. And did you touch anything while you were in the room, either of you?'

'Oh no.'

'Did you happen to notice, ma'am, whether there was paper in the typewriter?'

'There wasn't,' said Miss Marple. 'I noticed that at once because it seemed strange. Mr Gulbrandsen was sitting at the typewriter so he must have been typing something. Yes, I thought it very strange.'

Inspector Curry looked at her sharply. He said, 'Did you talk with Mr Gulbrandsen while he was here?'

'Very little.' Miss Marple thought. 'He asked me about Mrs Serrocold's health. In particular, about her heart.'

'Her heart? Is there something wrong with her heart?'

'Nothing whatsoever, I understand.'

Inspector Curry was silent for a moment or two, then he said, 'Mr Gulbrandsen left the group immediately after dinner, I understand?'

'Yes, he said he had a letter to write.'

'He didn't ask for a business meeting with Mr Serrocold?'

'No.' Miss Marple added, 'You see, they had already had one.'

'They had? When? I understood that Mr Serrocold only returned home just before dinner.'

'That's quite true, but he walked through the gardens, and Mr Gulbrandsen went out to meet him and they walked up and down the terrace together.'

'Who else knows this?'

'I don't think anybody else,' said Miss Marple. 'I just happened to be looking out of my window.'

'You didn't,' Inspector Curry said delicately, 'happen to overhear anything of what they said?'

Innocent blue eyes met his. 'Only bits, I'm afraid,' said Miss Marple gently. 'I do not know the actual subject of their conversation, but they wanted to save Carrie Louise from knowing something. To save her – that was how Mr Gulbrandsen put it, and Mr Serrocold said, "I agree that we must consider her." They also mentioned a "big responsibility" and that they should, perhaps, "take outside advice".'

She paused. 'I think you should ask Mr Serrocold himself about all this.'

'We will do so, ma'am. Now is there anything else that you thought unusual this evening?'

Miss Marple thought for a moment. 'It was all so unusual, if you know what I mean. But there was one thing. Mr Serrocold stopped Mrs Serrocold from taking her medicine. Miss Bellever was quite annoyed about it.' She smiled modestly. 'But that, of course, is such a little thing.'

'Yes. Well, thank you, Miss Marple.'

As Miss Marple went out of the room, Sergeant Lake said, 'She's old, but she's very observant.'

Chapter 10

Lewis Serrocold came into the study and sat down, not in the chair Miss Marple had just left, but in his own chair behind the desk.

He looked at the two police officers thoughtfully. He had the face of a man who was suffering badly in very difficult conditions, and it surprised Inspector Curry because, though Christian Gulbrandsen's death must have been a shock, Gulbrandsen had not been a close friend or relation. He was only a rather distant connection by marriage.

Lewis Serrocold said with a sigh, 'How difficult it is to know the right thing to do.'

'I think we will be the judges of that, Mr Serrocold,' said Inspector Curry. 'Now, Mr Gulbrandsen arrived unexpectedly, I understand?'

'He did.'

'And you have no idea of why he came?'

Lewis Serrocold said quietly, 'Oh yes, I know why he came. He told me.'

'Business connected with the Gulbrandsen Institute, I suppose?'

'Oh no, it was nothing to do with the Gulbrandsen Institute.' Lewis Serrocold continued seriously. 'I fully realize that with Gulbrandsen's murder, I have got to put all the facts before you. But I am worried about my wife's happiness and peace of mind. It is not for me to direct you, Inspector, but if you can find a way to keep certain things from her I would be grateful. You see, Inspector Curry, Christian Gulbrandsen came here to tell me that he believed my wife was being slowly and <u>cold-bloodedly poisoned</u>.'

'What?' Curry leaned forward, astonished.

Serrocold nodded. 'Yes, it was, as you can imagine, a huge shock to me. I had no suspicion of such a thing myself, but as soon as Christian told me, I realized that the symptoms of arthritis that my wife had complained of lately – pain in the legs and sickness – were also the symptoms of arsenic poisoning.'

'You definitely think, then, that Gulbrandsen's suspicions were correct?'

'Oh yes. He would not have come to me with such a suggestion unless he was sure of his facts. He was a careful man, and very thorough.'

'What was his evidence?'

'We had no time to discuss it. Our interview was hurried. It was only long enough to explain his visit, and to come to an agreement that nothing should be said to my wife.'

'And who did he suspect?'

'He did not say, and I don't think he knew. But he must have suspected – otherwise why would he be killed?'

'He mentioned no name to you?'

'No. He suggested that we ask for the advice of Dr Galbraith, the Bishop of Cromer. Dr Galbraith is one of the trustees, a man of great wisdom and experience who would support my wife if – if it was necessary to tell her of our suspicions.'

'How extraordinary,' said Curry.

'Gulbrandsen left us after dinner to write to Dr Galbraith. He was actually typing the letter when he was shot.'

'How do you know?'

Lewis said calmly, 'Because I have the letter here.' He took out a folded typewritten sheet of paper and handed it to Curry.

The Inspector said sharply, 'You shouldn't have touched anything.'

'I know I was wrong to move this, but I had a very strong reason. I felt certain that my wife would insist on coming into the room and I was afraid that she might read what is written here. And I would do anything – anything – to avoid my wife being unhappy.'

Inspector Curry said no more for the moment. He read the typewritten sheet.

Dear Dr Galbraith,

Please come to Stonygates as soon as you receive this. I am in the middle of an extraordinary crisis and I do not know how to deal with it. I know how strong your affection is for our dear Carrie Louise, and how serious your concern will be for anything that affects her. How much does she have to know? How much can we keep from her? Those are the questions that I find difficult to answer.

I have reason to believe that this sweet and innocent lady is being poisoned. I first suspected this when

Here the letter stopped.

Curry said, 'But why on earth was this letter in the typewriter and not taken by the murderer?'

'I can only guess that the murderer may have heard someone coming and only had time to escape.'

'How do you think this poison is being given?'

'It seems to me that the most likely answer is the medicine that my wife is taking. We all share the same food, but anyone could add arsenic to the medicine bottle.'

'We must have the medicine tested.'

Lewis said quietly, 'I already have a sample. I took it this evening before dinner.'

From a drawer in the desk he took out a small bottle with a pink liquid in it.

Inspector Curry said with a curious look, 'You think of everything, Mr Serrocold.'

'I acted immediately. Tonight, I stopped my wife from taking her usual dose. It is still in a glass in the Hall – the bottle of medicine itself is in the dining room.'

Curry lowered his voice. 'You'll excuse me, Mr Serrocold, but just why are you so anxious to keep this from your wife? Surely, for her own sake, it would be best if she were warned.'

'Yes – yes, that may well be so. But I don't think you understand. My wife, Inspector Curry, is an idealist, a completely trustful person. She has no idea of evil. She simply could not believe that someone would want to kill her. But it is not just "someone". It is a case – surely you see that – of someone very near and dear to her.'

'So that's what you think?'

'We have got to face facts. Close by we have a couple of hundred young delinquents who have been violent. But none of them can be a suspect in this case. By the very nature of things, a slow poisoner is someone living in the family. Think of the people who are here in this house; her husband, her daughter, her granddaughter and her husband, her stepson whom she regards as her own son, Miss Bellever her devoted friend. All very near and dear to her – and yet we must be suspicious that it is one of them.'

Curry said slowly, 'There are outsiders.'

'Yes, Dr Maverick and one or two of the staff are often with us, and the servants – but what possible motive could they have?'

Inspector Curry said, 'And there's young Edgar Lawson?'

'Yes. But he has only been here a short time.'

'But he's unbalanced. What about this attack on you tonight?'

Serrocold waved it aside impatiently. 'He had no intention of harming me. It was play-acting, no more.'

'Rather dangerous play-acting, Mr Serrocold.'

'You really must talk to our psychiatrist, Dr Maverick. He'll give you the professional view. Edgar will probably be quite normal tomorrow morning.'

'You don't wish to bring a charge against him?'

'That would be the worst thing possible. In any case, poor Edgar certainly did not shoot Gulbrandsen. He was in here threatening to shoot me.'

'That's the point I was coming to, Mr Serrocold. Anyone, it seems, could have come in from outside and shot Mr Gulbrandsen, as the terrace door was unlocked. But with what you have been telling me, the question is: who inside the house could have killed Mr Gulbrandsen?'

Lewis Serrocold said slowly, 'I can only tell you that everyone except the servants was in the Great Hall when Christian left it, and whilst I was there, nobody left it.'

'Nobody at all?'

'I think,' Lewis frowned, 'oh yes. Some of the lights went out – Mr Walter Hudd went to see to it.'

'That's the young American gentleman?'

'Yes – of course I don't know what took place after Edgar and I came in here.'

'And you can't be clearer than that, Mr Serrocold?'

Lewis Serrocold shook his head. 'No, I'm afraid I can't help you. It's – it's just not believable.'

Inspector Curry sighed. 'You can tell everyone that they can all go to bed. I'll talk to them tomorrow.'

When Serrocold had left the room, Inspector Curry said to Lake, 'Well – what do you think?'

'He knows – or thinks he knows, who did it,' said Lake.

'Yes. I agree with you. And he doesn't like it at all.'

Chapter 11

Gina greeted Miss Marple with a rush of words as she came down to breakfast the next morning. 'The police are here again. They're in the library this time, they're going to speak to everybody. I think the whole thing's horrible. I hate it. And Jolly's very bad tempered,' Holding on to her arm, Gina took Miss Marple into the dining room. 'I think it's because the police are in charge and Jolly can't "manage" them like she manages everybody else.

'Alex and Stephen,' continued Gina severely, as she saw the two brothers finishing their breakfast, 'just don't care.'

'Gina dearest,' said Alex, 'you are most unkind. Good morning, Miss Marple. I care very much. Except for the fact that I hardly knew your Uncle Christian, I'm obviously the best suspect.'

'Why?'

'Well, I was driving up to the house at the right time. And they've been checking on things – it seems that I took too much time between the gate and the house – time enough, apparently, to leave the car, run round the house, go in through the side door, shoot Christian and rush back to the car again.'

'And what were you really doing?'

'I stood for several minutes looking at the fog in the car's headlights and thinking what I would use to get that effect on a stage. For my new "Limehouse" ballet.'

'But you can tell them that!'

'Oh, you know what policemen are like. They have doubting minds.'

'It would amuse me to see you in trouble, Alex,' said Stephen with his rather cruel smile. 'Now, I'm all right! I never left the Hall last night.'

Gina cried, 'But they couldn't possibly think it was one of us!' Her dark eyes were upset.

Miss Bellever looked in at the door and said, 'Miss Marple, when you have finished your breakfast, will you go to the library?'

'Hey, what was that?' asked Alex.

'I didn't hear anything,' said Stephen.

'It was a gun shot.'

'They've been firing shots in the room where Uncle Christian was killed,' said Gina. 'I don't know why. And outside, too.'

* * *

Lewis Serrocold was standing by the window in the library. He turned and came forward to meet Miss Marple. 'I hope,' he said, 'that the shock has not made you ill. To be close to murder must be terrible for anyone who has not come in contact with such a thing before.'

Modesty stopped Miss Marple from replying that she was, by now, used to murder. She said that life in St Mary Mead was not so quiet as outside people believed.

Lewis Serrocold was not really listening. He said, 'I want your help.'

'But of course, Mr Serrocold.'

'I think that you have a real affection for my wife?'

'Yes, indeed. Everyone has.'

'That is what I believed. It seems that I am wrong. With the permission of Inspector Curry, I am going to tell you something that no one else knows. Or perhaps I should say what only one person knows.'

He told her what he had told Inspector Curry the night before about Carrie being poisoned.

Miss Marple looked horrified. 'I can't believe it, Mr Serrocold. I really can't.'

'That is what I felt when Christian Gulbrandsen told me.'

'Surely, dear Carrie Louise does not have an enemy in the world.'

'It seems impossible to believe that she does. But you understand, poisoning – slow poisoning – it must be one of our family.'

'If it is true.'

'The police tested Carrie Louise's medicine bottle and a separate sample of its contents. There was arsenic in both of them.'

Miss Marple said softly, 'So Ruth was right!'

'Ruth?'

Lewis Serrocold sounded surprised. Miss Marple's face turned pink. 'I did not come here by chance.'

Lewis Serrocold listened whilst Miss Marple told him of Ruth's concern. Then he said grimly, 'Well, it seems she was right. Now, Miss Marple, you see my problem. Should I tell Carrie Louise?'

Miss Marple said quickly, 'Oh no,' in an unhappy voice.

Lewis nodded. 'So you feel as I do? As Christian Gulbrandsen did. Would we feel like that with an ordinary woman?'

'Carrie Louise is not an ordinary woman. Her trust in people controls her whole life. I do feel that until we know who . . .'

'Yes, but you do see, Miss Marple, that there is a risk in saying nothing.'

'And so you want me to – to watch over her?'

'You are the only person I can trust,' said Lewis Serrocold simply.

'Because I only arrived a few days ago?' said Miss Marple.

Lewis Serrocold smiled. 'Exactly.'

'It is an unpleasant question,' said Miss Marple apologetically. 'But who exactly would benefit if dear Carrie Louise were to die?'

'Money!' said Lewis bitterly. 'It always comes back to money, doesn't it?'

'Well, I think it must be in this case. Because Carrie Louise is a lovely person, and one cannot imagine her having an enemy. But as you know, Mr Serrocold, people will often do anything for money.'

'I suppose so, yes.' He continued, 'Naturally Inspector Curry has already taken up that point. Mr Gilfoy is coming down from London today. His company wrote both Carrie Louise's <u>will</u> and the original will of Eric Gulbrandsen. My understanding is that Eric Gulbrandsen, after financing the College and his other charitable works, left equal amounts to Mildred and Pippa. He left the remainder of his fortune in a <u>trust fund</u>, the income to be paid to Carrie Louise for her lifetime.'

'And after her death?'

'It was to be divided equally between Mildred and Pippa – or their children if they had died before Carrie Louise.'

'So it goes to Mrs Strete and to Gina.'

'Yes. Carrie Louise has also a large fortune of her own. Half of this she gave to me four years ago. Of the remaining amount, she left ten thousand pounds to Juliet Bellever, and the rest equally divided between Alex and Stephen Restarick, her two stepsons.'

'Oh dear,' said Miss Marple. 'That means everyone in this house had a financial motive.'

'Yes. And yet, you know, I can't believe that any of these people would commit murder. I simply can't. Mildred is her daughter – and already well provided for. Gina is devoted to her grandmother. Jolly Bellever is totally devoted to Carrie. The two Restaricks care for Carrie Louise as though she were really their mother. And a lot of Carrie's income has been used to finance their theatrical work – especially so with Alex. I simply can't believe either of them would poison her. I just can't believe any of it, Miss Marple.'

'Not that it helps,' said Miss Marple. 'But actually to commit a murder, I think you need courage as well – or perhaps, more often, just conceit. Yes, conceit. I wondered . . .' She broke off as Inspector Curry came into the room.

Chapter 12

Lewis Serrocold went away, and Inspector Curry sat down and gave Miss Marple a rather knowing smile. 'So Mr Serrocold has been asking you to keep a close eye on his wife,' he said.

'Well, yes. I hope you don't mind.'

'I think it's a very good idea. Does Mr Serrocold know just how well qualified you are for the job?'

'I don't quite understand, Inspector.'

'He thinks you're just a very nice elderly lady who was at school with his wife.' He shook his head. 'We know you're more than that, Miss Marple, aren't you? You're very familiar with crime. Mr Serrocold only knows one part of it – the beginners, these juvenile delinquents. It makes me sick. There are plenty of good young men about, boys who are working hard. A good start in life would make a lot of difference to them. But there it is, honesty has to be its own reward – millionaires don't leave trust funds to help the good young people. Well, I've seen boys – and girls – with everything against them, bad homes, bad luck, every disadvantage, and they've had the determination to succeed, despite all their problems. That's the kind of person I will leave my fortune to, if I ever have one. But then, of course, I never will have a fortune. Just my pension and a nice bit of garden.' He nodded at Miss Marple. 'Superintendent Blacker told me about you last night. He said you've had a lot of experience of the bad side of human nature. Well now, let's have your view. Who killed Gulbrandsen? The American husband?'

'That,' said Miss Marple, 'would be very convenient for everybody.'

Inspector Curry smiled to himself. 'And his manner doesn't help. So, who's been poisoning Mrs Serrocold?'

'Well,' said Miss Marple, 'my first idea, human nature being what it is, is to think of the husband. Or, if it's the husband being poisoned, then the wife. That is always the first thought, don't you think, in a poisoning case?'

'I agree with you every time,' said Inspector Curry.

'But really – in this case –' Miss Marple shook her head. 'No, I cannot seriously consider Mr Serrocold. Because you see, Inspector, he really is devoted to his wife. It's very quiet, but it's genuine. He loves his wife, and I'm certain that he wouldn't poison her.'

'And he has no motive. She's given her money to him already.'

'I'm really afraid,' Miss Marple sounded rather sorry about it, 'we shall have to exclude him as a suspect.'

'No easy answer for us,' said the Inspector, smiling. 'And anyway, he couldn't have killed Gulbrandsen. It seems certain to me that whoever is poisoning Mrs Serrocold killed Gulbrandsen to prevent him talking. What we've got to decide now is who had an opportunity to kill Gulbrandsen. And our first suspect – there's no doubt about it – is young Walter Hudd. It was he who switched on a reading lamp which resulted in a fuse breaking, giving him the opportunity to leave the hall. It was while he was away from the Great Hall that the shot was heard. So that's suspect number one.'

'And suspect number two?' asked Miss Marple.

'Alex Restarick, who was alone in his car between the gate and the house and took too long getting there.'

'Anybody else?' Miss Marple leaned forward eagerly.

'Now that's where,' said Inspector Curry, 'I've got to ask you. You were there, in the Hall last night, and you can tell me who left it.'

'Yes – yes, I ought to be able to tell you – but can I? You see – the circumstances . . .'

'You mean that you were all listening to the argument going on in Mr Serrocold's study.'

Miss Marple nodded in complete agreement. 'Yes, we were all very frightened. Edgar Lawson really looked mad. Apart from Mrs Serrocold, who was calm, we all feared that he would hurt Mr Serrocold. He was shouting, you know, and saying the most terrible things – and what with that and with most of the lights being out – I didn't really notice anything else.'

'You mean that whilst that scene was going on, anybody could have left the Hall, shot Mr Gulbrandsen and come back again?'

'I think it would have been possible.' Miss Marple considered. 'But I can say that Mrs Serrocold did not leave – because I was watching her. It surprised me, you know, that she was able to remain so calm.'

'And the others?'

'Miss Bellever went out – but I am almost sure that was after the shot. Mrs Strete? I really don't know. She was sitting behind me. Gina was over by the far window. I think she stayed there the whole time, but I cannot be sure. Stephen was at the piano, but he stopped playing when the argument began.'

'So we can only exclude those people who did not have the opportunity. That's Lewis Serrocold and young Edgar Lawson in the study, and Mrs Serrocold in the Hall. It's very unfortunate, of course, that Gulbrandsen should be shot on the same evening that this trouble happened between Serrocold and young Lawson.'

'Just unfortunate, you think?' said Miss Marple.

'Oh? What do you think?'

'I did wonder,' said Miss Marple, 'if it had been planned.'

'So that's your idea?'

'Well, everybody seems to think it very strange that Edgar Lawson's condition should suddenly get worse. He says that

Churchill, Montgomery, or any famous man he happens to think of is his unknown father. But suppose somebody suggested that it is Lewis Serrocold who is really his father; Lewis Serrocold who has been working against him – that he is really the heir to Stonygates. In his weak mental state he would accept the idea – become more and more angry and then make the kind of scene he did. And what a wonderful cover that would be! Everybody would have their attention fixed on the dangerous situation – especially if somebody had thoughtfully supplied him with a gun.'

'Hmm, yes. Walter Hudd's gun.'

'Oh yes,' said Miss Marple, 'I had thought of that. But you know, Walter does not say much and he's certainly bad-tempered, but I don't think he's stupid.'

★ ★ ★

Two hours later Inspector Curry pushed back his chair, stretched himself and sighed. 'Well,' he said, 'we've cleared a lot of people.'

Sergeant Lake agreed. 'The servants are not suspects. They were together at the time.'

Curry nodded. He was tired. He had interviewed the therapists, the teachers, and the 'young delinquents' who were eating with the family that night. All their stories matched. They had all given each other alibis.

Dr Maverick had agreed with his staff, there had been no breaks in the College security. Christian Gulbrandsen could not have been killed by any of the 'young patients,' as Curry almost called them – it really was hard work holding on to good sense against the complete certainty of all these medical people.

And it was not a lot easier dealing with the family.

Chapter 13

Alex Restarick talked a lot. He also waved his hands about. 'I know, I know! I'm the best suspect. I drove here alone and on the way I had a creative thought. I do not expect you to understand. How could you?'

'I might,' Curry said, but Alex Restarick rushed on.

'It's just one of those things! They come to you – there's no knowing when or how. An idea – and everything else goes out of your mind! I'm producing *Limehouse Nights* next month. Suddenly – last night – it was wonderful. The perfect lighting. Fog – the way the car headlights lit the fog so brightly and yet there was nothing to be seen, the buildings just disappeared. Everything helped to create the right atmosphere! The shots – the running footsteps. And I thought – that's it – but how am I going to get these effects . . .'

Inspector Curry interrupted. 'You heard shots? Where?'

'Out of the fog, Inspector.' Alex waved his hands. 'Out of the fog. That was the wonderful part about it.'

'You didn't think that anything was wrong?'

'Wrong? Why should I?'

'Are shots so usual?'

'Ah, I knew you wouldn't understand! The shots fitted into the scene I was creating. I wanted shots, danger. What did I care what they were really? Someone shooting rabbits? I was imagining myself in Limehouse – or rather in the theatre – looking at Limehouse.'

'How many shots?'

'I don't know,' said Alex carelessly. 'Two or three. Two close together, I do remember that.'

Inspector Curry nodded. 'And the sound of running footsteps? Where were they?'

'They came to me out of the fog. Somewhere near the house.'

Inspector Curry said gently, 'That would suggest that the murderer of Christian Gulbrandsen came from outside.'

'Of course. Why not? You don't really suggest, do you, that he came from inside the house?'

Still very gently Inspector Curry said, 'We have to think of everything.'

Chapter 14

It was very difficult, Inspector Curry thought, to get a true understanding of someone from what other people said. Several people had described Edgar Lawson that morning, but looking at him now, Curry's own view was very different.

Edgar did not seem 'strange' to him or 'dangerous,' or 'self-important' or 'not normal'. He seemed a very ordinary and rather sad young man, sorry for himself and sorry for what he had done.

He was only too anxious to apologize. 'I've done wrong. I don't know what happened to me – really I don't. Making all that trouble – shooting off a gun. At Mr Serrocold too, who's been so good to me and so patient, too.'

He twisted his hands nervously – thin hands, with bony wrists. 'If I've got to go to prison, I deserve it. I'm guilty.'

'No charge has been made against you,' said Inspector Curry. 'According to Mr Serrocold, shooting the gun was an accident.'

'That's because he's so good. There never was a man as good as Mr Serrocold! He's done everything for me. And I repay him by acting like this.'

'What made you act as you did?'

Edgar looked embarrassed. 'I made a fool of myself.'

Inspector Curry said, 'So it seems. You told Mr Serrocold that he was your father. Was that true?'

'No, it wasn't.'

'What put that idea into your head? Did someone suggest it to you?'

'Well, it's hard to explain.'

Inspector Curry said in a kindly voice, 'Suppose you try.'

'Well, you see, I had a rather hard time as a kid. The other boys were bad to me – because I don't have a father. Mum was usually drunk and the house was always dirty, it was horrible. And then I started thinking, supposing my Dad was not just some sailor, but someone important – and I started to make up things. Then I went to a new school and I tried it once or twice, saying things. I said my father was really an officer in the Navy. I started believing it myself. I didn't feel so bad then. I thought up some other ideas. I got all mixed up. I couldn't stop telling lies.'

Inspector Curry nodded. He had already seen Edgar's police record.

'Mr Serrocold took me away from all that and brought me down here. He said he needed a secretary to help him – and I did help him! I really did. Only the others laughed at me. They were always laughing at me.'

'What others? Mrs Serrocold?'

'No, she's lovely – she's always gentle and kind. No, but Gina treated me like dirt. And Stephen Restarick. And Mrs Strete thought I was just a lying little thief! So did Miss Bellever!'

Curry noted that he was becoming more excited. 'So you didn't find them very kind?'

Edgar said passionately, 'If I had a proper father they wouldn't have behaved like that.'

'So you took a couple of famous fathers?'

Edgar blushed red. 'I always seem to end up telling lies.'

'And finally you said Mr Serrocold was your father. Why?'

'Because that would stop them, wouldn't it? If he was my father, they couldn't do anything to me.'

'Yes. But you told him he was your enemy.'

'I know –' The boy rubbed his head. 'I got things all wrong. There are times when I don't – when I don't get things right. I get mixed up.'

'And you took the gun from Mr Hudd's room?'

Edgar looked confused. 'Did I?'

'Don't you remember where you got it?'

Edgar said, 'It was just childish stuff.'

Inspector Curry said patiently, 'How did you get the gun?'

'You just said – out of Walter's room.'

'You remember doing that now?'

'I must have got it from his room. I couldn't have got it any other way, could I?'

'I don't know,' said Inspector Curry. 'Somebody might have given it to you?'

Edgar was silent – his face blank.

'Is that how it happened?'

Edgar said passionately, 'I don't remember. I was so angry. I walked around the garden in a terrible state. I thought people were watching me, trying to hurt me. I can't understand it all now. I feel I must have been mad. I don't remember where I was and what I was doing half the time!'

'Surely you remember who told you Mr Serrocold was your father?'

Edgar gave the same blank stare. 'Nobody told me. It just came to me.'

Inspector Curry sighed. He was not satisfied. But he judged he would get no more at the moment.

As Edgar went, Inspector Curry shook his head.

'Do you think he's mad, sir?' Sergeant Lake asked.

'Much less mad than I had imagined. Come on, Lake, I want to do a thorough <u>reconstruction</u> of the scene in the Hall.'

* * *

'That's a fact then.' Inspector Curry was sitting at the piano. Sergeant Lake was in a chair by the window overlooking the lake.

Curry went on, 'If I'm watching the study door, I can't see you.'

Sergeant Lake rose and went quietly through the door to the library.

'All this side of the room was dark. The only lights were the ones beside the study door. No, Lake, I didn't see you go. Once in the library, you could go out through the other door to the corridor – two minutes to run along, shoot Gulbrandsen and come back to your chair by the window. And Mrs Strete, she was close to the door to the hall that leads to all the other rooms, and it's a very dark corner. She could have gone and come back. Yes, it's possible.'

Curry grinned suddenly. 'And I could go.' He got off the music stool and went along the wall and out through the door. Coming back, he said, 'The only person who might notice I wasn't still at the piano would be Gina Hudd. And you remember what Gina told us: "Stephen was at the piano to begin with. I don't know where he was later".'

'So you think it was Stephen?'

'I don't know who it was,' said Curry. 'It wasn't Edgar Lawson or Lewis Serrocold or Mrs Serrocold or Miss Jane Marple. But for the rest,' he sighed, 'it's probably the American. Those fused lights were a bit too convenient. And yet, you know, I like him.' The Inspector was looking down at the old-fashioned music stool. He lifted the top. 'Still, that isn't evidence . . .' He stopped – lying on the pages of sheet music, was a small automatic gun.

'Stephen Restarick,' said Sergeant Lake joyfully.

'Not so fast,' Inspector Curry warned him. 'I believe that's just what we're meant to think.'

Chapter 15

As Carrie Louise came down the main staircase, three people met her: Gina, Miss Marple, and Juliet Bellever.

Gina spoke first. 'Darling!' she exclaimed passionately. 'Are you all right? The police haven't threatened you, have they?'

'Of course not, Gina. What a strange idea! Inspector Curry was most kind.'

'So he should be,' said Miss Bellever. 'Now, Carrie, I've got all your letters here and a parcel.'

'Bring them into the library,' said Carrie Louise.

All four of them went into the library. Carrie Louise sat down and began opening her letters. There were about twenty or thirty of them.

As she opened them, she handed them to Miss Bellever, who sorted them into piles, explaining to Miss Marple, 'There are three main types. One – from relations of the boys. Those I give to Dr Maverick. Letters asking for money I reply to myself. And the rest are personal – and Carrie gives me notes on how to deal with them.'

The letters finished, Mrs Serrocold turned to the parcel. Inside was an attractive box of chocolates. 'Someone must think it's my birthday,' said Mrs Serrocold with a smile. She opened the box. Inside was a visiting card. Carrie Louise looked at it in surprise. '"With love from Alex",' she read. 'How strange for him to post me a box of chocolates on the day he was coming here.'

Miss Marple felt a sudden uneasiness. She said quickly, 'Wait, Carrie Louise. Don't eat one yet.'

Mrs Serrocold looked even more surprised.

'Wait while I ask – Is Alex here, Gina?'

'He was in the Hall just now, I think.' She went across, opened the door, and called him.

Alex Restarick appeared in the doorway. 'My darling! It is so good to see you looking as well as this.' He came across to Mrs Serrocold and kissed her gently on both cheeks.

Miss Marple said, 'Carrie Louise wants to thank you for these chocolates.'

Alex looked surprised. 'But I never sent you any chocolates, darling.'

'The box has got your card in,' said Miss Bellever.

Alex looked down. 'So it has. How very strange. I certainly didn't send them.'

'They look very good' said Gina. 'Look, Grandma, there are your favourite cherry liqueur ones.'

Miss Marple gently took the box away from her. Without a word she left the room and went to find Lewis Serrocold. She found him in Dr Maverick's room in the College. She put the box on the table in front of him. As he listened to her, his face grew hard.

'We must get them tested for poison immediately,' said Dr Maverick.

'It seems incredible,' said Miss Marple. 'Everyone in the house might have been poisoned!'

Lewis nodded. His face was still white and hard. 'Yes. This is – it is not human –'

Miss Marple said quietly, 'If there is poison in these chocolates, then I'm afraid Carrie Louise will have to know what is going on. She must be warned.'

Lewis Serrocold said heavily, 'Yes. She will have to know that someone wants to kill her. I think that she will find it almost impossible to believe.'

Chapter 16

'Miss, is it true, Miss, there's a poisoner at work?'

Gina pushed the hair back from her face. There was paint on her cheek and on her trousers. She and her helpers had been busy on or their next theatrical production.

It was one of these helpers who was now asking the question. Ernie, the boy who had given her such valuable lessons in opening locks, was also a very good wood worker.

His eyes now were bright with pleasure. 'Everyone's talking about it,' he said. 'But it wasn't one of us, Miss. Not a thing like that. Nobody would hurt Mrs Serrocold. What poison was it, Miss?'

'I don't know what you're talking about, Ernie.'

Ernie shut one eye in a wink. 'Oh yes, Miss! Mr Alex it was who did it, so they say. He brought those chocolates down from London. But that's a lie. Mr Alex wouldn't do a thing like that, would he, Miss?'

'Of course he wouldn't,' said Gina.

'You really see life here!' Ernie said. 'Old Gulbrandsen murdered yesterday and now a secret poisoner. Do you think it's the same person doing both? What would you say, Miss, if I told you I know who it was who killed him?'

'You can't possibly know.'

'Oh, can't I? Supposing I was outside last night and saw something.'

'How could you have been out? The College is locked up at seven, after everybody has been checked in.'

'I can get out whenever I like, Miss. Locks don't mean anything to me. I can get out and walk around the grounds just for the fun of it, I can.'

Gina said, 'I wish you would stop telling lies, Ernie.'

'Who's telling lies?'

'You are. Telling stories about things you've never done at all.'

'That's what you say, Miss. You wait till the police come round and ask me all about what I saw last night.'

'Well, what did you see?'

'Ah,' said Ernie, 'wouldn't you like to know?'

Gina moved quickly to catch Ernie. Sensibly, Ernie ran off.

'The boys all seem to know about Grandma and the chocolates,' Gina told Stephen, as they walked back to the house that evening. 'And they knew about Alex's card. Surely it was stupid to put Alex's card in the box when he was actually coming here?'

'Yes, but who knew he was coming? It was a last minute decision. Probably, by the time his telegram arrived, the box was posted. And it would have been a good idea. Because he does send Carrie Louise chocolates.' He went on slowly, 'What I simply can't understand is . . .'

'Is why anyone would want to poison Grandma,' Gina interrupted. 'I know. I just can't believe it! Absolutely everyone loves her.'

Stephen did not answer.

Gina looked at him sharply. 'I know what you're thinking, Steve!'

'I wonder.'

'You're thinking that Walter – isn't very happy with her. But Walter would never poison anyone. The idea's laughable.' Gina went on hurriedly, 'Do you think Ernie was lying? He was pretending he was walking about in the fog last night, saying he could tell things about the murder. Do you think that might be true?'

'True? Of course not. You know he'll say anything to make himself important.'

★ ★ ★

The setting sun lit the west side of the house, with its terrace and steps leading down to the lawns.

'Is this where you stopped your car last night?' Inspector Curry asked, looking towards the house.

'Near enough,' Alex Restarick agreed. 'It's difficult to tell exactly because of the fog. Yes, I would say this was the place.'

Coming out from a covering of thick bushes, the drive turned here in a slow curve through a line of trees and then went on between the lake and the house.

'Dodgett,' said Inspector Curry.

Police Constable Dodgett started off immediately and ran as fast as he could across the lawn towards the house. Reaching the terrace, he went in by the side door. A few moments later the curtains of one of the windows were violently shaken. Then Constable Dodgett reappeared out of the garden door, and ran back to them, breathing very hard.

'Two minutes and forty-two seconds,' said Inspector Curry, holding up his stop-watch. 'They don't take long, these things, do they?' His tone was pleasantly conversational.

'I don't run as fast as your Constable,' said Alex. 'Are you timing my supposed movements?'

'I'm just pointing out that you could have done the murder. That's all, Mr Restarick.'

Alex Restarick said kindly to Constable Dodgett, who was still not breathing normally, 'I can't run as fast as you, but I believe I'm fitter.'

'I had bronchitis last winter,' said Dodgett.

Alex turned back to the Inspector. 'Seriously, in spite of trying to frighten me and watch my reactions, you can't believe I had anything to do with this?' Alex Restarick obviously found the idea very funny. 'I would not send a box of poisoned chocolates to Mrs Serrocold and put my card inside, would I?'

'That might be what we are meant to think, Mr Restarick.'

'Oh, I see. How clever. By the way, were those chocolates poisoned?'

'Yes. They contained aconitine.'

'Not one of my favourite poisons, Inspector. Personally, I prefer curare.'

'Curare has to be put into the bloodstream, Mr Restarick, not into the stomach.'

'How well informed the police are,' said Alex.

Inspector Curry looked sideways at the young man, seeing eyes that were full of laughter. A trickster with brains – that's how he would sum up Alex Restarick. In Inspector Curry's opinion, if Alex Restarick had murdered Gulbrandsen, he would be a very satisfactory criminal. But unfortunately Curry did not think he had.

'I moved the curtains as you told me, Sir,' Constable Dodgett said, having recovered his breath. 'And counted thirty. I noticed a hole in the top of the curtains. It means you would see the light in the room from outside.'

Inspector Curry said to Alex, 'Did you notice light from that window last night?'

'I couldn't see the house because of the fog. I told you. Well, the main part, that is. The gymnasium building, being closer, showed in a marvellous way. I could not see it as a solid building because of the fog, but I did see how I could use it to make a perfect illusion of dock warehouses. As I told you, I am putting on a show set in the London Docks: Ballet.'

'You told me,' agreed Inspector Curry.

'You know, because of my job I do look at things from the point of view of a theatre stage set, rather than from the point of view of reality.'

'I'm sure you do. And yet a stage set is real enough, isn't it, Mr Restarick?'

'I don't see what you mean, Inspector.'

'Well, it's made of real materials – cloth and wood and paint. The illusion is in the eye of the audience, not in the set itself. The set, as I say, is real enough, as real behind the scenes as it is in front.'

Alex stared at him. 'Now that, you know, is a very interesting comment, Inspector. It's given me an idea.'

'For another ballet?'

'No, not for another ballet. Dear me, I wonder if we've all been rather stupid?'

Chapter 17

'You say somebody has been trying to poison me?' Carrie Louise was simply unable to accept the idea. 'You know,' she said, 'I really can't believe it.'

Lewis said gently, 'I wish I could have protected you from this, dearest.'

She stretched out a hand to him and he took it.

Miss Marple, sitting close by, shook her head sympathetically.

'Is it really true, Jane?' Carrie Louise asked.

'I'm afraid so, my dear.'

'Then everything . . .' Carrie Louise stopped. She continued, 'I've always thought I knew what was real and what was not. This doesn't seem real – but it is. So I may be wrong everywhere. But who could want to do such a thing to me? Nobody in this house could want to – kill me.'

'That's what I would have thought,' said Lewis. 'I was wrong.'

'And Christian knew about it? That explains it.'

'Explains what?' asked Lewis.

'His behaviour,' said Carrie Louise. 'It was very strange, you know. Not like him. He seemed – upset about me. And he asked me if my heart was strong, and if I'd been well lately. But why not say something straight out? It's so much simpler.'

'He didn't want to cause you pain, Carrie.'

'Pain? But why – Oh, I see.' Her eyes widened. 'So that's what you believe. But you're wrong, Lewis, quite wrong. I am sure of that.'

Her husband avoided her eyes.

'I'm sorry,' said Mrs Serrocold after a moment or two. 'But I can't believe anything that has happened lately is true. Edgar shooting at you. That silly box of chocolates. It just isn't true.'

Nobody spoke.

Caroline Louise Serrocold sighed. 'I suppose,' she said, 'that I must have ignored everything but my own beliefs for a long time. Please, both of you, I think I would like to be alone. I've got to try to understand.'

★ ★ ★

Miss Marple came down the stairs and into the Great Hall to find Alex Restarick standing near the large entrance door, with his hand held out in a theatrical way.

'Come in, come in,' said Alex happily. 'I'm just thinking about last night.'

Lewis Serrocold, who had followed Miss Marple down from Carrie Louise's sitting room, crossed the Great Hall to his study and shut the door.

'Are you trying to reconstruct the crime?' asked Miss Marple with pleasure.

'No, not exactly,' Alex said. 'I was looking at the whole thing from an entirely different point of view. I was thinking of this place like it was a theatre. Just come over here. Think of it as a stage set with lights, actors entering and leaving, noises off stage. All very interesting. It wasn't all my own idea. The Inspector gave it to me. I think he's rather a cruel man. He did his best to frighten me this morning.'

'And did he frighten you?'

'I'm not sure.' Alex described the Inspector's experiment and the timing of the performance of the breathless Constable Dodgett. 'Time,' he said, 'is so very misleading. You think things take such a long time, but really, of course, they don't.'

'No,' said Miss Marple. What had Carrie Louise meant, she wondered, when she had said to her husband, 'So that's what you believe – but you're wrong, Lewis!'

'I must say that was a very clear-sighted remark of the Inspector's,' Alex's voice interrupted her thoughts. 'About a stage set being real. Made of wood and cloth and as real on the unpainted as on the painted side. "The illusion," he pointed out, "is in the eyes of the audience."'

'Like magicians,' Miss Marple said. 'They do it with mirrors is, I believe, what people say.'

Stephen Restarick came in, slightly out of breath. 'Hello, Alex,' he said. 'That little rat, Ernie Gregg, remember him? He's been telling Gina that he gets out at night and wanders about the gardens. He says he was wandering round last night and he saw something.'

Alex turned quickly. 'Saw what?'

'He says he's not going to tell. Actually I'm sure he's only trying to show off and get himself noticed. He does tell lies a lot, but I thought perhaps the police should question him.'

Alex said sharply, 'Why don't we leave him for a bit and not let him think we're too interested?'

'Perhaps – yes, I think you may be right there. This evening, perhaps.'

Stephen went on into the library.

Miss Marple, walking gently round the Hall, thinking of herself as an audience moving around a stage set, walked into Alex Restarick as he stepped back suddenly.

Miss Marple said, 'I'm so sorry.'

Alex frowned at her, said in an absent-minded sort of way, 'I beg your pardon,' and then added in a surprised voice. 'I was thinking of something else – that boy Ernie.' He made strange movements with both hands.

Then, with a sudden change of behaviour, he crossed the hall and went through the library door, shutting it behind him.

The sound of voices came from behind the closed door, but Miss Marple hardly noticed them. She was not interested in Ernie. She was sure that Ernie had seen nothing at all. She did not believe for a moment that on a cold foggy night like last night, Ernie would have used his abilities to open a lock so he could wander about in the gardens. It was most likely that he never got out at night. Showing off, that was all it had been.

'Like Johnnie Backhouse,' thought Miss Marple, who always had a parallel experience of life as an example, and all selected from the people of St Mary Mead.

"I saw you last night" had been Johnnie Backhouse's unpleasant comment to all he thought it might affect. It had been a surprisingly successful remark. So many people, Miss Marple thought, have been in places where they are anxious not to be seen!

She stopped thinking about Johnnie and concentrated on something which Alex had said, thoughts which had begun with some comments by Inspector Curry. Those remarks had given Alex an idea. Had they given her an idea, too? The same idea – or a different one?

She stood where Alex Restarick had stood. She thought to herself, 'This is not a real hall. This is only cloth and wood. This is a stage scene.' Bits of phrases flashed across her mind: illusion . . . in the eyes of the audience . . . they do it with mirrors . . . yards of coloured ribbon . . . vanishing ladies . . . all the show and misdirection . . . the magician's skill.

Something came into her mind – a picture – something that Alex had said, something that he had described to her; Constable Dodgett trying to get his breath back. Something moved in her mind and came suddenly into focus.

'Why of course!' said Miss Marple. 'That must be it.'

Chapter 18

Miss Marple was standing at the place where Inspector Curry had made his experiment with Constable Dodgett.

Miss Bellever's voice behind her startled her. 'You'll catch a cold, Miss Marple, standing about like that after the sun's gone down.'

Miss Marple walked obediently alongside her and they went quickly towards the house.

'I was thinking about magic tricks,' said Miss Marple. 'So difficult when you're watching them to see how they're done, and yet, once they are explained, so very simple. Did you ever see the *Lady Who is Cut in Half* – such an exciting trick? It fascinated me when I was eleven years old, I remember. And I never could think how it was done. But the other day there was an article in some paper explaining exactly how they do it. I don't think a newspaper should do that, do you? It seems it's not one girl – but two. The head of one and the feet of the other. You think it's one girl and it's really two – and the other way round would work equally well, wouldn't it?'

Miss Bellever looked at her with surprise. Miss Marple was not often so vague and unconnected as this. 'It's all been too much for the old lady,' she thought.

'When you only look at one side of a thing, you only see one side,' continued Miss Marple. 'But everything fits in perfectly well if you decide what is reality and what is illusion.' She added suddenly, 'Is Carrie Louise all right?'

'Yes,' said Miss Bellever. 'She's all right, but it must have been a shock, you know – discovering that someone wanted to kill her. I mean particularly a shock to her, because she doesn't understand violence.'

'Carrie Louise understands some things that we don't,' said Miss Marple thoughtfully. 'She always has.'

'I know what you mean – but she doesn't live in the real world.'

'Doesn't she?'

Miss Bellever looked at her in surprise.

Just then Edgar Lawson passed them, walking very fast. He gave a kind of embarrassed greeting, then looked away.

'I remember now who he reminds me of,' said Miss Marple. 'A young man called Leonard Wylie. His father was a dentist, but he got old and blind and his hand used to shake, and so people preferred to go to the son. But the old man was very miserable about it, said he was no good for anything any more. Leonard, who was very soft-hearted and rather foolish, began to pretend he drank more than he should. He always smelt of whisky. His idea was that his patients would go back to the father again.'

'And did they?'

'Of course not,' said Miss Marple. 'What happened was what anybody with any sense could have told him would happen! The patients went to Mr Reilly, the other dentist. So many people with good hearts have no sense. Besides, Leonard Wylie was so <u>unconvincing</u>. His idea of drunkenness wasn't in the least like real drunkenness, and he overdid the whisky – spilling it on his clothes in an impossible way.'

They went into the house by the side door.

Chapter 19

They found the family in the library. Lewis was walking up and down, and there was a sense of tension.

'Is anything wrong?' asked Miss Bellever.

Lewis said, 'Ernie Gregg is missing. Maverick and some of the staff are searching the grounds. If we cannot find him, we must call the police.'

'Grandma!' Gina ran over to Carrie Louise, worried by the whiteness of her face. 'You look ill.'

'I am so unhappy. The poor boy.'

Lewis said, 'I was going to question him this evening to find out if he had actually seen anything last night. I have the offer of a good job for him and I thought that after discussing that, I would mention the other matter.'

Miss Marple said softly, 'Foolish boy. Poor foolish boy.' She shook her head, and Mrs Serrocold said gently, 'So you think so too, Jane?'

Stephen Restarick came in. 'Hello, what's happening?'

Lewis repeated his information, and as he finished speaking, Dr Maverick came in with a fair-haired boy with pink cheeks and a suspiciously innocent expression. Miss Marple remembered him being at dinner on the night she had arrived at Stonygates.

'I've brought Arthur Jenkins along,' said Dr Maverick. 'He seems to have been the last person to talk to Ernie.'

'Now, Arthur,' said Lewis Serrocold, 'please help us if you can. Where has Ernie gone?'

'I don't know, sir. Honestly, I don't. He didn't say anything to me, he didn't. He was all excited about the play at the theatre, that's all.'

'There's another thing, Arthur. Ernie said he was wandering about the grounds after lock-up last night. Was that true?'

'Never! What a liar! Ernie never goes out at night. He used to say he could, but he wasn't that good with locks! Anyway he was in last night, that I do know.'

The door was thrown open and looking very pale and ill, Mr Baumgarten, the occupational therapist, came in. 'We've found him – them. It's horrible.' He sank down on a chair.

Mildred Strete said sharply, 'What do you mean – found them?'

Baumgarten was shaking. 'Down at the theatre,' he said. 'Their heads crushed – the big counterweight must have fallen on them. Alex Restarick and that boy Ernie Gregg. They're both dead.'

Chapter 20

'I've brought you a cup of soup, Carrie Louise,' said Miss Marple. 'Now please drink it.'

Mrs Serrocold sat up in the big bed. She looked very small and childlike. Her cheeks had lost their pink flush, and her eyes seemed very far away. She took the soup obediently. 'First, Christian,' said Carrie Louise, 'and now Alex – and poor, silly little Ernie. Did he really know anything?'

'I think he was just telling lies,' Miss Marple said as she sat down in a chair beside the bed. 'Making himself important by saying he had seen something. But somebody believed his lies.' Carrie Louise shivered. Her eyes went back to their far away look.

'We meant to do so much for these boys. We did do something. Some of them have done wonderfully well. Several of them are in really responsible jobs. A few failed – that can't be helped. Modern life is so complicated – too complicated for some simple and undeveloped characters. You know Lewis's great scheme? He always felt that transportation was a thing that had saved many criminals in the past. They were shipped overseas – and they made new lives in simpler surroundings. He wants to start a modern programme like that. He wants to buy a group of islands, to finance it for some years, then make it a self-supporting co-operative – with everyone taking a share in it. But far away from the bad old ways of the cities. It's his dream. But it will take a lot of money.'

Miss Marple picked up a little pair of scissors and looked at them closely. 'What a strange pair of scissors,' she said. 'They've got two finger holes on one side and one on the other.'

Carrie Louise's eyes came back from that frightening far distance. 'Alex gave them to me this morning,' she said. 'They're supposed to make it easier to cut your right hand nails. Dear boy, he was so enthusiastic. He made me try them.'

'And I suppose he collected the nail clippings and took them away,' said Miss Marple.

'Yes,' said Carrie Louise. 'He . . .' She stopped. 'Why did you say that?'

'I was thinking about Alex. He had brains. Yes, he had brains.'

'You mean – that's why he died?'

'I think so – yes.'

'He and Ernie.'

And then Carrie Louise said quietly and unexpectedly, 'How much do you know, Jane?'

Miss Marple looked up quickly. The eyes of the two women met.

Miss Marple said slowly, 'If I was quite sure.'

'I think you are sure, Jane.'

'What do you want me to do?' Jane Marple asked.

Carrie leaned back against her pillows. 'It is in your hands, Jane – You'll do what you think right.' She closed her eyes.

'Tomorrow,' Miss Marple hesitated, 'I shall have to try and talk to Inspector Curry – if he'll listen.'

Chapter 21

Miss Marple stood in the Great Hall and asked the Inspector to stand beside her. 'It's something I want to show you. Something Alex Restarick made me see. It's a question of magic tricks. They do it with mirrors, you know – that sort of thing – if you understand me.'

Inspector Curry did not understand. He wondered if Miss Marple was quite right in the head.

'I want you to think of this place as a stage set, Inspector. As it was on the night Christian Gulbrandsen was killed. You're here in the audience, looking at the people on the stage. Mrs Serrocold and myself and Mrs Strete, and Gina and Stephen – and just like on the stage there are entrances and exits and the characters go out to different places. Only, when you're in the audience, you don't think where they are really going. They go out "to the front door" or "to the kitchen" and when the door opens you see a little bit of painted scenery. But really of course they go out to the sides of the stage – or the back of the stage with carpenters and electricians, and other characters waiting to come on. They go out – to a different world.'

'I don't quite see, Miss Marple.'

'Oh, I know – I suppose it sounds very silly – but if you think of this as a play and the scene is "the Great Hall at Stonygates" – what exactly is behind the scene? I mean – what is behind the stage? The terrace – isn't it? The terrace and a lot of windows opening on to it.

'And that, you see, is how the magic trick was done. It was the trick of the Lady Cut in Half that made me think of it.'

'The Lady Cut in Half?' Inspector Curry was now quite sure that Miss Marple was mad.

'A most exciting magic trick. You must have seen it – only not really one girl but two girls. The head of one and the feet of the other. It looks like one person and is really two. And so I thought it could equally be the other way about. Two people could be really one person.'

'Two people really one?' Inspector Curry looked desperate.

'Yes. Not for long. How long did your Constable take in the garden to run to this house and back? Two minutes and forty-five seconds, wasn't it? This would be less than that. Well under two minutes.'

'What was under two minutes?'

'The magic trick. The trick when it wasn't two people but one person. In there – in the study. We're only looking at the visible part of the stage. Behind the scenes there is the terrace and a row of windows. So easy when there are two people in the study to open the study window, get out, run along the terrace – those footsteps Alex heard – in at the side door, shoot Christian Gulbrandsen and run back. During that time, the other person in the study does both voices so that we're all quite sure there are two people in there. And so there were most of the time, but not for that little period of under two minutes.'

Inspector Curry found his breath and his voice. 'Do you mean that it was Edgar Lawson who ran along the terrace and shot Gulbrandsen? Edgar Lawson who poisoned Mrs Serrocold?'

'But you see, Inspector, no one has been poisoning Mrs Serrocold at all. That's where the misdirection comes in. Someone very cleverly used the fact that Mrs Serrocold's pains from arthritis were not unlike the symptoms of arsenic poisoning. It's the old magician's trick of forcing a card on you. It is easy to add arsenic to a bottle of medicine – easy to add a few lines to a typewritten letter. But the real reason for Mr Gulbrandsen's coming here was the most likely reason – something to do with the Gulbrandsen Trust. Money, in fact. Suppose that there had been embezzlement – embezzlement on a very big scale – you see where that points? To just one person.'

Inspector Curry gasped, 'Lewis Serrocold?' he said in disbelief.

'Lewis Serrocold.' said Miss Marple.

Chapter 22

Part of a letter from Gina Hudd to her aunt Mrs Van Rydock:

– and so you see, darling Aunt Ruth, the whole thing has been just like a nightmare – especially the end of it. I've told you all about this funny man Edgar Lawson. He always behaved like a rabbit – and when the Inspector began questioning him and breaking him down, he lost his nerve completely and ran like a rabbit. He jumped out of the window and ran round the house and down the drive and there was a policeman waiting, and Edgar just turned to one side and ran full speed for the lake. He jumped into an old boat that has been lying there falling apart for years – and he pushed off. Quite a mad, senseless thing to do, of course, but as I say, he was just a rabbit in a panic. And then Lewis gave a great shout and said 'That boat's got a hole in it,' and raced off to the lake, too. The boat went down and there was Edgar struggling in the water. He couldn't swim. Lewis jumped in and swam out to him. He got to him but they were both in difficulty because they'd become caught among the reeds. One of the Inspector's men went in with a rope round him, but he got trapped in the reeds, too and they had to pull him out. Aunt Mildred said 'They'll drown – they'll drown – they'll both drown' in a silly sort of way, and Grandma just said 'Yes.' I can't describe to you just how she made that one word sound. Just 'YES' and it went through you like – like a knife.

Am I being silly and dramatic? I suppose I am. But it did sound like that.

And then – when it was all over, and they got them out, the Inspector came to us and said to Grandma, 'I'm afraid, Mrs Serrocold, there's no hope.'

Grandma said very quietly, 'Thank you, Inspector.'

Then she looked at us all. Me wanting to help, but not knowing how, and Jolly, looking grim and tender and ready to take care as usual, and Stephen reaching out his hands, and funny old Miss Marple looking so sad, and tired, and even Walter looking upset. All so fond of her and wanting to do SOMETHING.

But Grandma just said 'Mildred.' And Aunt Mildred said 'Mother.' And they went away together into the house, Grandma looking so small and frail and leaning on Aunt Mildred. I never realized, until then, how fond of each other they were. It didn't show much, you know, but it was there all the time.

Gina paused and sucked the end of her pen. She started again:

About me and Walter – we're coming back to the States as soon as we can.

Chapter 23

'What made you guess, Jane?'

Miss Marple took her time before answering. She looked thoughtfully at the other two – Carrie Louise, thinner and frailer and yet strangely untouched – and the old man with the sweet smile and the thick white hair. Dr Galbraith, Bishop of Cromer.

The Bishop took Carrie Louise's hand in his. 'This has been a great sadness for you, my poor child, and a great shock.'

'Sadness, yes, but not really a shock.'

'No,' said Miss Marple. 'That's what I discovered, you know. Everyone kept saying how Carrie Louise lived in another world from this and was out of touch with reality. But actually, Carrie Louise, it was reality you were in touch with, and not the illusion. You are never fooled by illusion like most of us are. When I suddenly understood that, I saw that I must trust what you thought and felt. You were quite sure that no one would try to poison you, you couldn't believe it – and you were quite right not to believe it, because it wasn't so! You never believed that Edgar would harm Lewis – and again you were right. He never would have harmed Lewis.

'So therefore, if I was to go by you, all the things that seemed to be true were only illusions. Illusions created for a reason – in the same way that magicians create illusions, to trick an audience. *We* were the audience.

'Alex Restarick got an idea of the truth first because he had the chance of seeing things from a different angle – from the outside angle. He was with the Inspector in the drive, and he looked at the house and realized the possibilities of the windows – and he remembered the sound of running feet he had heard that night, and then the timing of the Constable showed him what a very short time things take. The Constable got very breathless, and later, thinking of that, I remembered that Lewis Serrocold was out of breath that night when he opened the study door. He had just been running hard, you see.

'But it was Edgar Lawson that was the centre of it all to me. There was always something wrong to me about Edgar Lawson. All the things he said and did were exactly right for what he was supposed to be, but he himself wasn't right. Because he was actually a normal young man playing the part of a schizophrenic – and he was always a little more theatrical than is true to life.

'It must have all been very carefully planned. Lewis must have realized when Christian last visited that something had made him suspicious. And he knew that if Christian suspected anything, then he would not stop until he had discovered the whole truth.'

Carrie Louise said, 'Yes, Christian was like that. I don't know what it was that had made him suspicious but he started investigating – and he found out the truth.'

The Bishop said, 'I blame myself for not having been a better trustee.'

'Nobody expected you to understand finance,' said Carrie Louise. 'Lewis's great financial experience gave him complete control. And it was a test of honesty that he failed.' The pink colour came up in her cheeks. 'Lewis was a great man,' she said. 'A man of great vision, and a passionate believer in what could be done – with money. He didn't want it for himself – or at least not in the greedy sense – he did want the power of it – he wanted the power to do great good with it.'

'And so he embezzled the trust funds?' said Miss Marple.

Dr Galbraith hesitated. 'It wasn't only that.'

'Tell her,' said Carrie Louise. 'She is my oldest friend.'

The Bishop said, 'Lewis Serrocold was what one might call a financial expert. In his years of highly technical accountancy, he had amused himself by working out various methods of embezzlement which were almost impossible to detect. This had just been a game for his own entertainment, but then he saw what could be done with a huge sum of money. And it stopped being a game. You see, he had some first-class material to use. Amongst the boys who passed through here, he chose a small select group. They were boys who were naturally criminal, who loved excitement and who were very intelligent. We still don't know everything, but it seems clear that this group was specially trained and were placed in key positions. By carrying out Lewis's directions, very large sums of money were stolen without anybody being suspicious. I understand that the operations are so complicated that it will be months before they can all be uncovered. But the result seems to be that, under various names and banking accounts and companies, Lewis Serrocold would have been able to control a huge sum of money. He was going to establish an overseas colony where juvenile delinquents would eventually come to own and rule the place as a co-operative. It may have been a wild dream.'

'It was a dream that might have come true,' said Carrie Louise.

'Yes, it might have come true. But the means Lewis Serrocold used were dishonest, and Christian Gulbrandsen discovered that. He was very upset, particularly by what the discovery and prosecution of Lewis would mean to you, Carrie Louise.'

'That's why he asked me if my heart was strong, and seemed so worried about my health,' said Carrie Louise. 'I couldn't understand it.'

'Then Lewis Serrocold returned,' the Bishop continued, 'and Christian met him outside the house and told him that he knew what was happening. Lewis took it calmly, I think. Both men agreed they must do all they could to save you from the pain this knowledge would bring you. Christian said he would write to me and ask me to come here, as a co-trustee, to discuss the position.'

'But of course,' said Miss Marple, 'Lewis Serrocold had already prepared for this emergency. It was all planned. He had brought the young man who was to play the part of Edgar Lawson to the house. There was a real Edgar Lawson – of course – in case the police looked up his record. This false Edgar knew exactly what he had to do – act the part of a schizophrenic victim of persecution – and give Lewis Serrocold an alibi for a few vital minutes.

'The next step had been carefully planned too. Lewis's story that you, Carrie Louise, were being slowly poisoned, was very clever. There was nobody but Lewis who could say what Christian had told him – that, and a few lines he added on the typewriter while he was waiting for the police. It was easy to add arsenic to the medicine. No danger for you there – since he was ready to stop you drinking it. The chocolates were just an added touch – and of course the original chocolates weren't poisoned – only those he poisoned before giving them to Inspector Curry.'

'And Alex guessed,' said Carrie Louise.

'Yes – that's why he collected your nail clippings. They would show if arsenic actually had been given over a long period.'

'Poor Alex – poor Ernie.'

There was a moment's silence as the other two thought of Christian Gulbrandsen, of Alex Restarick, and of the boy Ernie – and the terrible act of murder.

'But surely,' said the Bishop, 'Lewis was taking a big risk in persuading Edgar to be his accomplice – even if he had some power over him –'

Carrie shook her head. 'It wasn't exactly a hold over him. Edgar was devoted to Lewis.'

'Yes,' said Miss Marple. 'I wonder perhaps if . . .' She paused delicately.

'You saw the likeness, I suppose?' said Carrie Louise.

'So you knew that all along?'

'I guessed. I knew Lewis had once had an affair with an actress, before he met me. I've no doubt at all that Edgar was actually Lewis's son.'

'Yes,' said Miss Marple. 'That explains everything.'

'And he gave his life for him in the end,' said Carrie Louise. She looked at the Bishop. 'He did, you know.'

There was a silence and then Carrie Louise said, 'I'm glad it ended that way with his life given in the hope of saving the boy from drowning. People who can be very good can be very bad, too. I always knew that was true about Lewis. But – he loved me very much – and I loved him.'

'Did you – ever suspect him?' asked Miss Marple.

'No,' said Carrie Louise. 'Because I was puzzled by the poisoning. I knew Lewis would never poison me and yet that letter of Christian's said definitely that someone was poisoning me – so I thought that everything I knew about people must be wrong.'

Miss Marple said, 'But when Alex and Ernie were found killed. You suspected then?'

'Yes,' said Carrie Louise. 'Because I didn't think anyone else but Lewis would have dared. And I began to be afraid of what he might do next.' She shivered. 'I admired Lewis. I admired his – what shall I call it – his goodness? But I do see that if you're good, you have to be humble as well.'

Dr Galbraith said gently, 'That, Carrie Louise, is what I have always admired in you – your humility.'

The lovely blue eyes opened wide in surprise. 'But I'm not particularly good. I can only admire goodness in other people.'

'Dear Carrie Louise,' said Miss Marple.

Character list

Ruth Van Rydock: a rich American, married and divorced three times; Carrie's sister

Miss Jane Marple: an elderly lady and close friend of the two sisters from their schooldays

Carrie Louise Serrocold: Ruth's sister, also wealthy, who lives at a house called Stonygates

Eric Gulbrandsen: Carrie Louise's first husband who died when she was thirty-two

Johnnie (John) Restarick: Carrie Louise's second husband who left her for a woman from Yugoslavia

Lewis Serrocold: Carrie Louise's third and present husband, an accountant and philanthropist who runs the Gulbrandsen Institute for young criminals at Stonygates

Pippa: the daughter Carrie Louise adopted with Eric Gulbrandson. She died in childbirth. She was married to Guido, an Italian aristocrat.

Mildred Strete: Carrie Louise and Eric Gulbrandson's natural daughter. A childless widow, who had married a senior priest (now dead) of the Church of England.

Gina Hudd: Pippa and Guido's daughter, brought up by her grandmother, Carrie Louise – married to Walter Hudd

Alex Restarick: elder son of Johnnie Restarick from his first marriage

Stephen Restarick: younger son of Johnnie Restarick from his first marriage

Edgar Lawson: assistant to Lewis Serrocold

Juliet (Jolly) Bellever: companion and secretary to Carrie Louise

Jackie Flint: one of the young criminals at the Institute

Walter Hudd: Gina's young American husband, an ex-Marine

Dr Maverick: a young psychiatrist

Mr Baumgarten: an occupational therapist

Christian Gulbrandsen: Carrie Louise's stepson and half-brother of Mildred, the principal trustee of the Institute

Inspector Curry: the police officer in charge of investigating the murder

Dr Galbraith: Bishop of Cromer and trustee of the Institute

Superintendent Blacker: Curry's superior officer

Sergeant Lake: a police officer assisting Curry

Ernie Gregg: one of the boy criminals being educated at Stonygates

Constable Dodgett: a police officer working with Curry and Lake

Mr Gilfoy: a trustee of the Institute and Carrie Louise's lawyer

Arthur Jenkins: a boy criminal at the Institute

Cultural notes

Philanthropic causes

People who were very rich and didn't have to work for money often liked to spend their time helping people who were not as lucky as they were. They did this by working for different charities or by setting up different philanthropic organizations. In the story, Carrie's first and last husbands were both interested in helping people in this way.

Education for all

Carrie's first husband, Mr Gulbrandsen, spent his time and his money trying to make important changes to the lives of people in Britain. One of these changes was the 'education for all' cause mentioned by Ruth at the beginning of the story. Gulbrandsen believed that everybody should be able to go to school, not just children younger than twelve, and the children of the rich, whose schooling was paid for by the parents. However, a series of laws were passed giving free education to every child. Before the war, free education was offered to children up until the age of twelve and, in 1944, until the age of fifteen, which meant that it was no longer necessary for people like Gulbrandsen to fight for this cause.

Juvenile delinquents

Another cause, this time one that Carrie's current husband, Lewis, was involved in at Stonygates was trying to help young people who had committed crimes. These people were officially called juvenile delinquents. Lewis believed that if you helped these young people, by teaching them how to do different jobs – and by giving them self-confidence – they would stop being criminals and would be able to live normal lives.

Children in the Second World War

At the beginning of the Second World War in Britain, everyone thought that the country was going to be invaded by the Germans and that all the major cities would be destroyed by bombs being dropped. People sent their children to the countryside where they would be safe. The children did not know where they were going to live or who their 'new families' would be. By the end of the war a total of 3.5 million people, most of them children, had been sent away from the towns and cities at some point during the war.

Many rich people, with the same idea of keeping their children safe, sent them to relatives abroad, which is why Gina in the story went to live with her Aunt Ruth in America.

Changes in the British class system

Up until the Second World War there was a strict and very clear class system in Britain. People got married to other people of the same social class; working class servants worked for the upper classes, the upper classes, especially women, didn't usually work at all; and everyone knew how they should behave. Because of the war, this all started to change. All the classes fought and died together; women started doing all the jobs that men had done previously – the men were all fighting in the war and someone had to do the work.

People fell in love and got married very quickly. They did not know if they were going to be killed fighting or have a bomb dropped on them at home and so the traditional class rules became less important. Before the war it was unusual for an upper-class girl like Gina to marry a man who had no money or profession, especially an American.

Winston Churchill and General Montgomery

In 1952, when this story was published, **Winston Churchill** had just become Prime Minister of Britain for the second time. The first time, 1940–1945, was during the Second World War. Churchill was famous during this time for the way he spoke to the people of Britain, both live and on the radio, encouraging them to be brave and not to even think that they would not win the war. Many people admired Winston Churchill and thought he was a good prime minister.

General Montgomery was an officer in the British army who became a General during the Second World War. He is probably the most famous British General from that time because he had key roles in many of the battles throughout the war. Many people admired him.

The trick of the Lady Cut in Half

The trick of the Lady Cut in Half is a popular magic trick where a woman or girl gets into a long rectangular box. The magician closes the box and at one end we can see the lady's feet and at the other we can see her head. The magician talks to the lady and asks her to move her feet, which she does and we see her talking and laughing. The magician covers the box with a cloth and cuts the box into two pieces and takes away the cloth. The lady is alive – talking and laughing and she moves her feet again even though they are now in another box.

The title of the story: *They Do It With Mirrors* is also connected to magicians and the tricks they do.

Glossary

Key

n = noun

v = verb

adj = adjective

adv = adverb

excl = exclamation

exp = expression

phr v = phrasal verb

absent-minded (adj)
someone who forgets things and doesn't pay attention to what they are doing is said to be absent-minded

accomplice (n)
a person who helps to commit a crime

accountancy (n)
the work of keeping financial records

accountant (n)
a person whose job is to keep financial records

aconitine (n)
a powerful **poison** made from herbs

affair (n)
a sexual relationship between two people who are married, but not to each other

affection (n)
feelings of love or liking for someone

alibi (n)
proof that you were somewhere else when a crime was committed, showing why you can't be guilty of a crime

arsenic (n)
a very powerful **poison**

arthritis (n)
condition in which the joints in someone's body are swollen and painful

at close range (exp)
being very close to something

awkward (adj)
embarrassing and difficult to deal with – an awkward person feels uncomfortable or clumsy

backfire (n)
an explosion in the exhaust pipe of a car that makes a loud noise

binoculars (n)
two small telescopes joined together side by side which you look through to see things that are far away

Bishop (n)
a religious leader of high rank

bitter (adj)
angry and resentful

break off (phr v)
to stop talking before you have said everything you were going to say

bring a charge (exp)
to accuse someone formally of having done something illegal

bronchitis (n)
an illness that makes you cough

Canon (n)
one of the religious leaders on the staff of a **cathedral**

case (n)
a person that a professional such as a doctor is dealing with

cashier (n)
the person in a bank that customers pay money to or get money from

cathedral (n)
a large important church which has a **Bishop** in charge of it

cause (n)
an aim which a group of people supports or is fighting for

charitable (adj)
helping and supporting people who are ill, disabled, or poor

cliff (n)
a high area of land with a very steep side, especially next to the sea

cold-bloodedly (adv)
doing something without showing pity or emotion

colony (n)
a group of people living together

companion (n)
when Agatha Christie was writing, a companion was usually someone who was paid to spend time with someone, often an elderly person

conceit (n)
the high opinion you have of yourself

confidential (adj)
spoken or written in secret and should stay secret

conspiracy (n)
the secret planning by a group of people to do something wrong or illegal

Constable (n)
a police officer in Britain of the lowest rank

co-operative (n)
a business or organization run by the people who work for it, who share its benefits and profits

counterweight (n)
a heavy object used in the theatre to balance scenery

crank (n)
a person who has strange ideas or behaviour

cruelty (n)
the act of deliberately causing pain or worry

curare (n)
a **poison** from South America

delicate (adj)
small and attractive

delicately (adv)
in a way that is sensitive to people's feelings

deprive (v)
to prevent someone from having something they want or need

devoted (adj)
caring for or loving something or someone very much

dignified (adj)
calm, impressive, and worthy of respect

dock warehouse (n)
a large building used for storing things at the place where ships are loaded

dose (n)
the amount of a medicine or a drug that should be taken at one time

earnest (adj)
serious and sincere

embezzlement (n)
stealing money from where you work, or from clients

evidence (n)
information from documents, objects, or witnesses, which is used in a court of law to try to prove something

fortune (n)
a very large amount of money

frail (adj)
very weak, not strong or healthy

fraud (n)
the crime of gaining money by a trick or lying

frown (v)
to move your eyebrows together because you are annoyed, worried, or thinking

fuse (n)
a **wire** which melts and stops the electric current if there is a fault

good grief (excl)
used to show great surprise

grim (adj)
unpleasant or serious

grin (v)
to smile widely

groan (v)
to make a long, low sound of pain or unhappiness

heir (n)
someone who has the right to receive a person's money, property, or title when that person dies

humble (adj)
not believing that you are better than other people

humility (n)
the quality of not believing that you are better than other people

hysterical (adj)
being in a state of uncontrolled excitement or panic

ideals (n)
ideas that you believe are right and worth trying to achieve

illegitimate (adj)
a person who is illegitimate was born of parents who were not legally married to each other

illusion (n)
something that appears to exist, but in reality does not exist or is something else

Inspector (n)
an middle ranking officer in the British police

invasion (n)
when a foreign army enters a country by force

irritably (adv)
doing something in a way that shows you are annoyed

juvenile delinquency (n)
when a young person behaves in a criminal way

knit (v)
to make something from wool using two knitting needles

knock someone out (phr v)
to make someone unconscious by hitting them hard on the head

landlady (n)
a woman who allows you to live or work in a building which she owns, in return for rent

lawn (n)
an area of grass that is kept cut short and is usually part of a garden or park

leper (n)
a person who has the disease leprosy, often kept separate from other people

live on (phr v)
to survive by eating only one type of food

loyally (adv)
showing support for a friend

mad about (adj)
very interested in something

Marine (n)
a soldier who is trained for duties at sea and on land

medal (n)
a small metal disc, given as an award for bravery

misdirection (n)
directing someone's attention away from what you are really doing

modestly (adv)
not showing your abilities, achievements, or possessions

motive (n)
the reason for doing something

nonsense (n)
something that you think is untrue or silly

nun (n)
a female member of a religious community

observant (adj)
when a person is good at watching other people and understanding them

occupational therapist (n)
a person who helps people recover from an illness by giving them activities to do

official inquiry (n)
a formal investigation by the police

pension (n)
money which a retired person regularly receives from a former employer

persecution (n)
when people are deliberately targeted to be harmed

philanthropic (adj)
giving money to people who are ill, disabled, or poor

plain (adj)
looking ordinary and not at all beautiful

poison (v)
to give people or animals something that harms or kills them if they swallow it

procedure (n)
the correct way of doing something

prosecute (v)
to charge someone with a crime and put them on trial

psychiatrist (n)
a doctor who is trained in the treatment of mental illness

psychologist (n)
a person who is trained in psychology, the study of how the mind works

purr (v)
to make the sound a cat makes in its throat when it is happy

reconstruction (n)
a description of a crime, which you make by trying to repeat it

reeds (n)
tall plants that grow in water

relish (n)
enjoyment

revenge (n)
the act of hurting someone who has hurt you

Riviera (n)
the French and Italian coast that was and is popular for tourism

sample (n)
a small amount of something that is examined and analyzed scientifically

schizophrenic (n)
someone who has the illness schizophrenia, a serious mental illness that prevents people from relating their thoughts and feelings to what is happening around them

Sergeant (n)
a police officer above the rank of **Constable**

show off (phr v)
to try to impress people by showing in a very obvious way what they can do or what they own

single-minded (adj)
not thinking about anything other than one thing

sly (adj)
clever at cheating people or hiding things from people

snap (v)
to speak in a sharp, unfriendly way

sobbing (n)
crying in a noisy way

spoilt (adj)
behaving badly because you have always had everything you want

spy (v)
to watch someone secretly

startle (v)
when something sudden and unexpected surprises you

statement (n)
something that you say or write which gives information in a formal or definite way

struggle (v)
to try to do something that is very difficult

suicide (n)
people who commit suicide deliberately kill themselves because they do not want to continue living

surgeon (n)
a doctor who performs operations

symptom (n)
a sign of an illness that shows you have that illness

tendency (n)
a worrying or unpleasant habit or action that keeps occurring

transportation (n)
the act of moving people from one place to another

trustee (n)
someone with legal control of money or property that is kept or invested for another person

trust fund (n)
money that is kept for someone and is used to make more money by investing it

unacknowledged (adj)
not recognized

unconvincing (adj)
if something is unconvincing, you do not believe it is true

victim (n)
someone who has been hurt or killed

vision (n)
strong ideas about how things might be different in the future

vivid (adj)
very bright in colour

wander (v)
to walk around with no direction

weed (n)
a wild plant growing where it is not wanted, for example in a garden

widow (n)
a woman whose husband has died

widower (n)
a man whose wife has died

will (n)
a document where you say what you want to happen to your money and property when you die

willpower (n)
a very strong determination to do something

wire (n)
a long, thin piece of metal that is used to fasten things or to carry electric current

wrinkled (adj)
having skin with a lot of lines on it

yard (n)
a unit of length equal to 36 inches or approximately 91.4 centimetres

Collins
English Readers

ALSO IN THE AGATHA CHRISTIE SERIES

Sparkling Cyanide

Six people sit down for dinner at a table laid for seven. No one can forget the night exactly a year ago that Rosemary Barton died at this same table surrounded by the same people, her beautiful face turned blue with cyanide poison.

Rosemary had always been memorable – and people had strong reactions to her. Did one of the six people at dinner feel strongly enough about her to kill her?

Crooked House

The Leonides family live together in a large and crooked house in a wealthy London suburb. When the elderly millionaire Aristide Leonides is murdered with a fatal injection, the family reluctantly suspect his glamorous, young second wife.

Charles Hayward, who is engaged to the late millionaire's granddaughter, observes the family closely and makes a terrible and shocking discovery . . .

They Came to Baghdad

Victoria Jones is a young English woman who is looking for love. She follows her new love interest to Baghdad, but she has no idea what adventure is waiting for her there.

A very important international meeting is planned in Baghdad, but a secret organization wants to sabotage it. Meanwhile, when a man dies in

Victoria's hotel room, he whispers three words to her: '. . . Lucifer . . . Basrah . . . Lefarge . . .' What do these words mean? And what does it have to do with the meeting?

A Pocket Full of Rye

Rex Fortescue, the boss of a financial empire, was sipping tea in his office, when he suffered a painful and sudden death. When the police checked the victim's pockets, they found grain.

Miss Marple knows one of the servants in Rex Fortescue's house and comes to help solve the mystery. She soon starts to suspect that she is dealing with a case of crime by rhyme . . .

After the Funeral

After Richard Abernethie's funeral, his will is read out to his family. His sister, Cora, shocks everyone by saying 'He was murdered, wasn't he?'

When Cora is murdered in her bed the very next day, her extraordinary remark suddenly seems very important.

Every member of the Abernethie family has something to gain from both murders. Hercule Poirot arrives to solve the mystery.

Destination Unknown

Famous scientists from around the world are disappearing and nobody knows why. The one woman who can help uncover the truth is dying after a plane crash. How can they discover where the scientists are without her?

Meanwhile, in a hotel room in Casablanca, Hilary Craven decides to end her life. But her suicide attempt is interrupted by a man who offers her an exciting alternative . . .

Hickory Dickory Dock

Strange items have disappeared from the student hostel on Hickory Road and Mrs Hubbard, the warden, is becoming suspicious.

Detective Hercule Poirot has been a little bored recently and decides to try to solve the mystery. But the investigation turns sinister when one of the students is found poisoned in her room.

4.50 From Paddington

A woman is murdered on a train.

When Miss Marple telephones her friend Lucy Eyelesbarrow and asks her to go undercover to investigate, Lucy quickly accepts the challenge!

Who is the dead woman? What was the motive for her murder? And why was the body thrown from the train and later hidden at Rutherford Hall?

When a second murder takes place, everyone at Rutherford Hall seems in danger, so Miss Marple sets a trap to catch the murderer.

Cat Among the Pigeons

Late one night, two teachers investigate a mysterious light in the school Sports Pavilion. Among the tennis racquets and lacrosse sticks, they find the body of the unpopular games mistress – shot through the heart.

Schoolgirl Julia Upjohn knows too much, and begins to worry that she might be the next victim. Can detective Hercule Poirot find the killer before the 'cat' strikes again?

The Agatha Christie Series

The Mysterious Affair at Styles
The Man in the Brown Suit
The Murder of Roger Ackroyd
The Murder at the Vicarage
Peril at End House
Why Didn't They Ask Evans?
Death in the Clouds
Appointment with Death
N or M?
The Moving Finger
Sparkling Cyanide
Crooked House
They Came to Baghdad
They Do It With Mirrors
A Pocket Full of Rye
After the Funeral
Destination Unknown
Hickory Dickory Dock
4.50 From Paddington
Cat Among the Pigeons

Visit **www.collinselt.com/agathachristie** for language activities and teacher's notes based on this story.